Cambridge Elements ☰

Elements in Psychology and Culture
edited by
Kenneth D. Keith
University of San Diego

GLOBAL CHANGES IN CHILDREN'S LIVES

Uwe P. Gielen
St. Francis College

Sunghun Kim
St. Francis College

CAMBRIDGE
UNIVERSITY PRESS

CAMBRIDGE
UNIVERSITY PRESS

University Printing House, Cambridge CB2 8BS, United Kingdom

One Liberty Plaza, 20th Floor, New York, NY 10006, USA

477 Williamstown Road, Port Melbourne, VIC 3207, Australia

314–321, 3rd Floor, Plot 3, Splendor Forum, Jasola District Centre, New Delhi – 110025, India

79 Anson Road, #06–04/06, Singapore 079906

Cambridge University Press is part of the University of Cambridge.

It furthers the University's mission by disseminating knowledge in the pursuit of education, learning, and research at the highest international levels of excellence.

www.cambridge.org
Information on this title: www.cambridge.org/9781108461634
DOI: 10.1017/9781108594011

First published 2019

A catalogue record for this publication is available from the British Library.

ISBN 978-1-108-46163-4 Paperback
ISSN 2515-3986 (online)
ISSN 2515-3943 (print)

Global Changes in Children's Lives

Elements in Psychology and Culture

DOI: 10.1017/9781108594011
First published online: December 2018

Uwe P. Gielen and Sunghun Kim
St. Francis College

Abstract: This Element compares the nature of childhood in four representative societies differing in their subsistence activities: bands of Australian hunter-gatherers, Tibetan nomadic pastoralists, peasants and farmers residing in Maya villages and towns, and South Korean students growing up in a digital information society. In addition, the Element traces a variety of intertwined global changes that have led to sharply reduced child mortality rates, shrinking family sizes, contested gender roles, increased marriage ages, long-term enrollment of children (especially girls) in educational institutions, and the formation of "glocal" identities.

Keywords: global childhood, Australian Aborigines, Tibetan nomads, Maya farmers, South Korean students

ISBNs: 9781108461634 (PB), 9781108594011 (OC)
ISSNs: 2515-3986 (online), 2515-3943 (print)

Contents

It is better to live for one day as a lion than for a thousand years as a sheep.

– Tibetan proverb

1 Introduction

During recent decades, much progress has been made in the scientific study of children and their varying environments across a broad spectrum of non-Western and Western societies. Relevant studies include those conducted by anthropologists, sociologists, demographers, economists, cross-culturally oriented psychologists, an increasing number of psychologists and other social scientists working in non-Western countries, members of nongovernmental organizations (NGOs) such as Save the Children interested in furthering the welfare of children in various parts of the world, important United Nations International Children's Emergency Fund (UNICEF) publications including the annual overview titled *The State of the World's Children*, and Max Roser's (2018c) extensive website, *Our World in Data*. It is our purpose to integrate some of these ecosocial, demographic, and sociocultural studies. In addition, it is our aim to present a selective overview of the world's 2.3 billion children and youth from a long-term, dynamic, and globally oriented perspective. The perspective highlights the joint impact of ecological, technological, economic, demographic, and sociocultural forces on children's lives. A major emphasis is placed on non-Western societies where more than 85% of all children live. However, this Element is less concerned with individual psychological differences, neither does it assess the cross-cultural validity of commonly discussed developmental theories such as Piaget's. Rather, its main focus is on the general nature of children's lives as these are shaped by diverse ecological and sociocultural contexts.

In order to provide sufficient ecological variety and context, we initially distinguish between four types of societies that rely on different kinds of subsistence activities: (1) small foraging bands of hunter-gatherers that until about 11,000–12,000 years ago were the only existing societies but that are now facing radical challenges and approaching extinction in their original forms; (2) nomadic pastoralists who herd livestock and seasonally move them to different pastures; (3) peasant societies whose populations are mostly engaged in farming based on formerly traditional but now evolving techniques; and (4) postindustrial, digital information societies that have made headway during recent decades especially in East Asia, Europe, North America, and Australia. We then describe in more detail the changing lives of children, adolescents, and their families in four evolving societies representing different forms of subsistence economy: Australian hunter-gatherers, Tibetan nomads, Maya peasants and farmers residing in Mexico and Guatemala, and education-obsessed modern South Korean families and their tech-savvy offspring. After discussing in some detail the broader contexts of childhood in these representative societies, we analyze some recent transformations in the nature of childhood both in these societies and around the globe. These include the rapid increase in the number of children in the world's poorer countries due to their rapidly declining mortality rates, the pervasive impact of schooling on the length, nature, and cultural meanings of childhood and adolescence, the declining prevalence and shifting nature of child work, and the effects of the digital revolution and globalization on the hybrid and "glocal" (both global and local) identities of many modern adolescents. Around the world societies are on the move, which means that the nature and sociocultural contexts of childhood are changing rapidly in many of them.

The average length of childhood in the narrow sense as well as of adolescence and youth varies considerably from society to society. Here, we pragmatically adopt the definition used by the United Nations' Convention on the Rights of the Child. In this important convention, the first international, legally binding, and comprehensive legal document protecting the rights of children, a child is defined as everybody prior to his or her eighteenth birthday (United Nations Assembly, 1989). Keep in mind, however, that in many nonindustrialized societies, both past and present, central aspects of a girl's childhood were or are only operative until she reaches her early to mid-teens. At that time, she is probably already fulfilling many adult duties and might even be married – or she might have been promised to an older man since her early years. In most preindustrial societies, girls experience greater continuity between childhood and adulthood than holds true for boys. Still, adolescence does display some universal biological, cognitive, and psychosocial features. Thus, preindustrial societies typically recognize some intermediate period between childhood and adulthood that acknowledges a person's physical and cognitive growth, sexual maturation, improving social skills, and ability to assume new responsibilities (Schlegel & Barry, 1991). Moreover, many preindustrial societies, such as various Australian Aboriginal societies and African age-graded societies, have established puberty-related initiation rituals designed to help young people deal with major changes in their lives as they approach adulthood. In contrast, modern adolescents are frequently among the first to be exposed to, and to selectively embrace, major technological and sociocultural changes. They are therefore of special interest when assessing the impact of globalization on the development of human behavior (Gibbons, 2000).

In the interest of arriving at an overall and dynamic picture of global childhood, we highlight the broad impact of subsistence activities, technological factors, modern health practices, schooling, changing family systems and gender roles, digitalization, and globalization on the lives of children.

In addition, for several societies, we discuss in some detail certain religious and other belief systems that are exerting a major influence on children's socialization practices. Several of our examples pertain to the children and families of minority groups such as Aboriginal groups in Australia, Tibetan nomads in China, and indigenous Maya in Guatemala and Mexico. Like many other nations, Australia, China, Guatemala, and Mexico are multiethnic countries that must face the difficult and ethically challenging task of integrating children and adults from a considerable range of cultural and linguistic backgrounds. Children from minority groups are frequently forced to struggle with economic and sometimes racial discrimination, linguistic challenges, educational institutions in which they may not feel at home, cultural differences conducive to multicultural identity conflicts, and discontinuities between their own lives and those led by their elders.

Approaches emphasizing the impact of ecological, demographic, economic, and technological factors tend to favor a more functional analysis of children's lives than those preoccupied with differences in cultural belief systems (Barry, Child, & Bacon, 1959). An example is that hunter-gatherer societies tend to have total fertility rates (TFRs) of four to eight children per woman per lifetime, whereas the rates of almost all postindustrial information societies in East Asia and Europe have now dropped below the fertility replacement rate of 2.1 children per woman per lifetime (UNICEF, 2017, table 4.1). One fundamental reason for this striking difference is that in traditional hunter-gatherer societies, only an average of 57% of all children survive up to age fifteen (Gurven & Kaplan, 2007: 326; see also Volk & Atkinson, 2013), whereas in postindustrial societies, the percentage hovers around 99%. Moreover, teenage girls in hunter-gatherer societies tend to get married around the age of twelve to eighteen years. This age is close to the time of their menarche, which tends to occur at an average age of eleven to seventeen years depending on a society's food supply and ecological circumstances. Once they become mothers, they breastfeed their children for two to four years and soon thereafter they are likely to get pregnant again. Despite this pattern, the overall population growth of such societies can be precarious and sometimes quite slow, in part because their fertility replacement rates typically exceed three children due to the prevailing high mortality rates for both children and adults. It is "functional" for the members of small foraging societies to culturally embrace their fertility-enhancing practices because if they do not, such societies will sooner or later die out. In contrast, women in postindustrial societies spend many years in school and tend to get married much later, commonly around a societal mean age of twenty-seven to thirty-two years (United Nations Population Division, 2017). Given that these women and their partners are surrounded by many millions of co-citizens and, not rarely, immigrants, they do not have to worry that their respective societies are going to become extinct anytime soon. Still, these societies are now aging and a few of them such as Japan have already begun to shrink in size. Moreover, in most pastoralist and peasant societies as well as in many hunter-gatherer bands, girls in particular begin to help out their parents around the ages of four to seven years, whereas in postindustrial societies, the practical contributions of most middle-class children to family survival are quite limited in scope. Indeed, modern parents typically find it quite expensive to bring up their children, adolescents, and "emerging adults" – and because of that, they are having fewer and fewer children (Kağıtçıbaşı & Ataca, 2005). This pattern holds true in culturally highly diverse countries such as Bosnia-Herzegovina (TFR in 2017 = 1.3), Italy (1.44), Singapore (0.83–1.16), and South Korea (1.26), all of which have very low birth rates almost never before seen in history (UNICEF, 2017, table 4.1).

Although this Element adopts a functional and long-term approach, this is not meant to imply that contradictory and dysfunctional practices are missing from the behavioral repertoires of most individuals and cultural groups. Indeed, motivational trade-offs within individuals and conflicts of interest between individuals or groups of individuals are unavoidable. For instance, it is of economic advantage for most modern adults to bring up only a few or maybe no children at all. However, that also means that prosperous societies such as Japan, Singapore, South Korea, and Taiwan are aging rapidly while unsuccessfully trying to convince their young women to marry earlier and to have more children. Thus, what might be economically functional for individual parents or single persons can be biologically dysfunctional for society at large. Moreover, having few, if any, children is clearly detrimental to the inclusive fitness of individuals when seen from an evolutionary perspective. Such a perspective emphasizes an individual's biologically anchored interest in transmitting his or her genetic blueprint to numerous descendants. Interesting, this also means that parents from religiously motivated groups emphasizing the desirability of bringing up many children (e.g., the Amish, Hassidim, Hutterites, Mennonites, and Mormons) are well adapted from a biological and evolutionary perspective. In contrast, politically progressive advocates focusing extensively on girls' education and gender equality in the worlds of work and politics tend to have fewer children and therefore lower levels of inclusive fitness. Such a trade-off, however, is only rarely discussed given the politically progressive rather than traditionally religious leanings of many social scientists. Moreover, at the global level, the morally laudable and increasingly successful campaigns to reduce child mortality rates especially in the poorer countries are nevertheless leading to historically unprecedented population increases. These are leading to dire long-term consequences for the deteriorating environment and for the intensifying climate crisis. Thus, the historical and ongoing changes in global patterns of childhood and adolescence have numerous – and, at times, quite difficult to reconcile – biological, moral, sociocultural, and political repercussions, a few of which are briefly touched on at the end of this Element.

In the following, we examine the impact of ecological differences and cultural blueprints on the lives of children in four highly varied and rapidly evolving types of societies.

2 Children's Lives in Four Contrasting Types of Societies

2.1 Four Kinds of Societies

Alongside many anthropologists, macro sociologists such as Lenski (2005) and Nolan and Lenski (2014) distinguish between different types of societies based on their predominant mode of subsistence and their access to various kinds of technologies. For Lenski, such types and subtypes of societies include hunting and gathering, fishing, horticultural, agrarian, maritime, herding, industrial, and postindustrial societies. Given that these societies do not always have neat and tidy boundaries, some of them evolve in a process of social evolution and grow into larger, increasingly stratified, and technologically more advanced societies. For instance, some of the advanced hunter-gatherer groups grew over time into either nomadic pastoralist or horticultural societies, or they were conquered or displaced by such societies. (Lenski defines horticultural societies as those that are based on domesticated plants and the use of hoes, digging sticks, and similar instruments. We use the term *peasant societies* for settled societies that employ a variety of agricultural technologies.) We have selected four kinds of societies for their contrasting characteristics, some of which are outlined in Table 2.1.

Small-scale foraging bands have presumably existed in some form for hundreds of thousands of years. Today they are changing, shrinking in number, and being pushed by larger and more powerful social groups into marginal desert and jungle areas (Codding, 2016). Foraging for plants and hunting various small and large animals, the members of these small-scale, low-density bands depend on a variety of family systems, gender roles, age categories, socialization practices, and religiously inspired worldviews as the basis of their social organization. They do not know specialized full-time occupations, although part-time healers such as shamans are commonly found among them. Whereas smaller, relatively egalitarian bands tend to lack layers of social stratification, some larger and more stratified hunting and gathering societies have probably

Table 2.1 Four Types of Society

	Small-scale foraging bands	Nomadic pastoralist societies	Peasant societies	Digital information societies
Examples	Australian Aborigines; !Kung (Kalahari Desert, Namibia, Botswana, South Africa); Aka Pygmies (Western Congo Basin)	Traditional Tibetan nomads (China/Tibet); Mongolian pastoralists (Mongolia); Dinka and Nuer pastoralists (South Sudan); traditional Navaho sheepherders (the United States)	Maya (Mexico, Guatemala); traditional rural villages and societies in Africa, Asia, preindustrial Western Europe, and the United States	Present-day South Korea, Japan, Singapore, Australia, New Zealand, most of Europe, Canada, the United States, Dubai
Average Population Size and Density	Small, fluid bands of fifteen to sixty seminomadic persons; very low population densities but compact settlements; bands form a part of larger cultural-linguistic groups	Small groups embedded in medium to large cultural groups; low to medium population densities; today increasingly embedded in large states	Villagers embedded in large to very large state societies with moderate to very high population densities	Very large, urbanized societies; very high population densities
Subsistence Activities and Economic Basis of Society	Foraging for roots, nuts, vegetables, fruits, honey,	Keeping and herding of animals such as goats, sheep, cattle, pigs,	Agriculture and subsistence farming; keeping of animals;	Information and service industries; manufacturing; smallish

	insects; hunting of small and big animals	horses, camels, lamas, and yak for dairy products, meat, pelts, transportation purposes, and sale	crafts; trade; today, migration to cities (including slums) is reinforcing basic socioeconomic changes	agricultural sector; local and international trade
Division of Labor and Socioeconomic Stratification	Limited to division by gender and age; part-time shamans; no or limited social stratification; emphasis on sharing; egalitarianism common	Moderate division of labor; e.g., herders, medical and religious specialists, traders, soldiers; stratification increases with size	Moderate division of labor; stratification and inequality moderate to extreme; societies becoming more heterogeneous	Extreme heterogeneity (more than 200,000 different job titles in the United States); pronounced stratification
Societal Complexity; Rural vs. Urban Areas	Small bands on the move displaying limited functional specialization mostly according to gender and age	Moderate complexity; life in tents common; increasing seasonal transhumance	Moderate complexity in rural areas; greater complexity in the urban areas	Very high complexity esp. in the widespread urban areas
Influence of Religion(s) and Supernatural Conceptions	Polytheistic religions often linked to environmental features and based on oral traditions	Polytheistic and monotheistic religions that may be based on sacred literature	Polytheistic and monotheistic religions; mixture of local beliefs and world religions based on sacred literature	Weakening influence of religion in Europe and East Asia; separation of church and state esp. in non-Islamic societies

Table 2.1 (cont.)

	Small-scale foraging bands	Nomadic pastoralist societies	Peasant societies	Digital information societies
Impact of External and Global Influences	Symbiotic relationships with pastoralists and agriculturalists; external and global influences increasing	Tensions with state authorities and agricultural groups common; global influences increasing	Indirect and direct impact that is increasing	Direct and pervasive impact especially in major cities and through mass media
Speed of Societal Change	Formerly slow but now rapidly increasing	Formerly slow and uneven but now rapidly increasing	Formerly slow and uneven but now steadily increasing	Very rapid
Balance between Tradition and Innovation	Traditions are/were emphasized but innovative influences are increasingly arriving from the outside	Traditions may be valued yet are losing ground	Traditions are emphasized but increasing exposure to innovation partially introduced from abroad	High rate of cultural change favors innovation over tradition; in many Islamic countries, tensions arise between tradition, modernity, and religious beliefs
Gender Roles	Clear differentiation of gender roles; women/girls tend to collect plants and small animals;	Gender roles sharply distinguished; girls do housework and milking while boys look after	Gender roles sharply distinguished and seen as part of the natural and sacred order; males	Contested and less differentiated gender roles; males more aggressive and assertive;

	while men/older boys hunt big game and defend the group; mixed gender playgroups in early childhood	large livestock and learn to fight; more freedom for boys, girls kept closer to home	more aggressive and assertive; more freedom for boys, girls kept closer to home; less extreme differences in matrilineal societies	gender roles perceived as human made and changeable; schooling increases female expectations, possibilities, and autonomy
Gender Inequality and Violence against Females	Low to moderate inequality and violence against women (but violence among Australian Aborigines, North American larger groups, and South American mixed horticultural-foraging societies)	Often pronounced in the widespread patrilineal and patrilocal societies; female infanticide and physical violence against women not uncommon	Patriarchal and hierarchical systems predominate; inequality and female infanticide and neglect common in patrilineal and patrilocal societies but less so in matrilineal and small societies	Increasing egalitarianism; neolocal rather than patrilocal residence favors more egalitarian husband–wife bonds; marital violence fairly common

existed for millennia in Australia, South and North America, and elsewhere. For those that rely on fishing as their main form of foraging, Lenski (2005) established a separate category of fishing societies. However, our focus here is on the lives of children in smallish, pedestrian, and more or less egalitarian bands, rather than on children growing up in larger, more stratified, and more sedentary fishing societies, or in larger North American societies that use horses, or in one of the many indigenous groups in the Americas that combine foraging with slash-and-burn horticulture (Roscoe, 2006).

Rather than living in villages, foraging bands create temporary shelters made from local resources such as tree branches or pieces of ice in the Arctic areas. Frequently on the move, they search for roots, nuts, vegetables, fruits, honey, insects, and eggs, and hunt both small and large animals. Embracing oral traditions and the power of environmental forces, their polytheistic religions often turn such forces into at times benign and at times threatening supernatural beings that must be placated. Most modern groups rely on economic relationships with agriculturalists, pastoralists, and nowadays information societies that increasingly serve as conduits for external and global influences (Hewlett & Lamb, 2005). Societal changes, which formerly occurred at a slow pace, are now accelerating and ubiquitous because of the introduction of new technologies, beliefs, and education systems. While men and women are socialized into clearly defined gender roles, early childhood is often characterized by mixed-gender playgroups. Women and girls tend to collect plants and small animals, while men and older boys hunt big game and are expected to defend the group should it become necessary. Inequality between the sexes tends to be low to moderate in the smaller groups, although it is more pronounced in some Australian societies (Jarrett, 2013). Violence occurs fairly frequently within, and between, some Australian Aboriginal groups as well as among larger groups residing in the Americas, but it is less prevalent among several small foraging groups residing in various Central African jungle areas (Hewlett & Lamb, 2005).

Nomadic pastoralists began to emerge around 8,000 years ago in the Fertile Crescent (today's southern Turkey, Iraq, Lebanon, Syria, Israel, and Palestine) and, sometime later, in Central Asian areas as well as the Tibetan Changtang, the world's highest and most extensive plateau. Depending on an area's ecology, pastoralists breed animals such as goats, sheep, cattle, horses, camels, llamas, alpacas, yaks, and reindeer. Today, an estimated 30 million pastoralists still follow this way of life while many others combine it with various forms of horticulture, agriculture, and, nowadays, the use of selected postindustrial technologies (Isom, 2009). Consequently, about a quarter of the world's land is used for grazing purposes. Nomadic pastoralists can be found in a considerable number of areas such as predominantly Tibetan areas in China (Miller, 2007), the extensive grasslands of Mongolia, some of the mountainous areas of Afghanistan, the savannas of Africa, certain high pasture regions in South America's Andes Mountains, and elsewhere. In earlier years, some groups of nomadic pastoralists, such as those living in Mongolia, periodically coalesced into large-scale tribes and societies led by charismatic and ruthless military and political leaders such as Genghis Khan (1162–1227). In a related vein, Ekvall (1961) argues that the nomadic patterns of living among the Tibetans can serve as a "preparation for war." In particular, boys are expected to be assertive and to acquire martial skills that may be required for defensive purposes but also for raiding excursions against agricultural and nomadic neighbors. Today, however, nation-states such as China are increasingly succeeding in keeping their Tibetan and other pastoralists under tight political, administrative, and military control. Other pastoralists, such as the cattle-herding Dinka and Nuer of South Sudan, however, are involved in at times deadly conflicts with each other.

Many nomadic pastoralist groups have fairly low to medium population densities that, however, are on the increase in modern nation-states. They exhibit moderate degrees of societal complexity as most of their members tend to live in small, local groups of tents. Once such groups settle down and get partially involved in agricultural pursuits, they often adopt a pattern of "seasonal transhumance" of their livestock between higher mountain pastures in the summer and lower valley pastures, together with permanent human residence, in the winter seasons (a form of agropastoralism).

The religions of pastoralists may be polytheistic or monotheistic. Some of them are based on sacred literature taught by religious specialists such as Tibetan and Mongolian lamas. Pastoralists mostly follow patrilineal and patrilocal traditions that tend to favor male power and inequality between the sexes. At times this may include physical violence against females. Gender roles are clearly distinguished, with the girls learning how to prepare food, milk animals, collect dung, and take care of small siblings from early on. The boys enjoy more freedom while learning to control and guard livestock against human and nonhuman predators (Hermanns, 1959). Various global and national influences are increasingly impacting the lives of nomadic pastoralists and modifying their lifestyles.

Agrarian forms of subsistence economy first began to evolve some 10,000–12,000 years ago in the Fertile Crescent region of the Middle East. Beginning about 6,000 years ago, and based on the cultivation of cereal and other crops, a variety of peasant societies and agriculturally based city-states developed at different times and more or less independently from each other in diverse regions of the world. This occurred in the Middle East, North Africa, Europe, East Asia, South and Southeast Asia, and Central and South America. Fully developed agrarian societies can support much higher population densities than societies based on hunting, gathering, nomadism, or simple gardening. This important characteristic, in turn, did over time lead to the formation of sometimes very large and systematically stratified states that have dominated most of recorded human history.

Peasant societies are based on villages and towns that in the course of time become embedded in state societies. In addition to subsistence farming, many traditional peasants keep animals, produce craft, and engage in local trade. Today, rural inhabitants are increasingly producing for the market as well. Comparable to many pastoralist societies, a moderate degree of division in labor tends to prevail in the smaller sections of agricultural societies. However, economic and social inequality among peasants/farmers and even more so between peasants/farmers and the political elites who rule their lives is often quite pronounced. Landless laborers and, in former times, slaves form(ed) the bottom layer of many agricultural societies. Comparable to the pastoralist societies, peasants may endorse either polytheistic or monotheistic religions based in part on sacred literature. Mixtures between local beliefs and practices and the official religion can be commonly found. Gender roles are considered natural and may assume a semi-sacred character. Boys enjoy more freedom than girls and tend to be more assertive and aggressive. Patriarchal institutions are customary, and inequality as well as female infanticide and neglect occur in quite a few patrilineal and patrilocal societies (Caldwell & Caldwell, 2005). However, gender inequality tends to be less pronounced in some of the smaller matrilineal and matrilocal societies that often rely on swidden horticulture. Today, national and global influences impact these societies both directly and indirectly, so if they once were slow to change, they are now undergoing more rapid transformations.

The main focus here is on Maya children and adolescents living in present-day villages and towns located in Guatemala, Mexico, and Belize (Kramer, 2005). In recent decades, a good many Maya villagers have been experiencing a shift from subsistence farming to cash-crop farming in tandem with many other changes such as wage labor, partial urbanization, better access to modern health care systems, expanded educational systems, access to two or more languages, and increased exposure to national and international ways of thinking (Goldin, 2011). Such developments are not only changing the lives of Maya children and adolescents in major ways but are also transforming the lives of families and their children in many other evolving peasant societies such as India (Seymour, 2010).

In the latter part of the eighteenth century, the Industrial Revolution took off in Great Britain but soon became influential in other Western countries and, less than a century later, in Japan. By the late twentieth century, rapidly evolving industrial technologies and associated ways of life had spread to many other parts of the globe, including several nations located in East Asia. Industrialized nations are based on the development of industrial technology and the application of mechanic or inanimate sources of energy to a steadily expanding range of production problems, including those found in the agricultural sector. In these societies, large sectors of the population are moving from the rural areas to burgeoning towns and cities. There, the inhabitants work in factories and growing service industries while increasingly occupying a very broad range of white collar positions.

By the late twentieth century, many industrialized societies were beginning to adopt intricate digital information and communication technologies and thus began to evolve into postindustrial, digital information societies. Within a few decades, the new technologies helped to transform those societies' economic, social, and cultural institutions and ways of life, while linking them more closely to other societies in an intensifying process of globalization. Some of these changes are especially visible in the lives of their adolescents. Given the widespread growth of the educational sector in modern postindustrial societies, their children and many of their youths are now attending educational institutions that tend to leave a decisive imprint on their daily lives, identities, psychological well-being, family relationships, and future plans. An extreme example of such a process can be found in modern South Korea (Seth, 2002). In these societies, many children and youth intend to become knowledge specialists rather than agricultural or industrial workers in the hope of getting better pay and leading easier lives.

Many digital information societies are very large in size and harbor densely packed populations in their expanding urban areas. Their economy is based on information and service industries, manufacturing, and extensive internal and international trade. Their agricultural sectors rely on highly mechanized farming methods and employ only a small percentage of the population. They are oriented toward production for local, national, and sometimes international markets. Societal complexity and heterogeneity tend to assume extreme degrees, especially in the urban sectors. However, such heterogeneity may undermine societal cohesion while at the same time the influence of religious traditions has been diminishing in parts of Europe, East Asia, and Latin America. The influence of rapid technological change and the forces of digitization favor innovation over cultural tradition in modern times, although selected traditions may remain viable once they undergo a process of redefinition and revitalization. In some Islamic countries, tensions between the forces of modernity and tradition have manifested themselves in the form of sometimes violent religious struggles among teenagers and adults. Digitalized societies allow for increased gender role diversity, and the expansion of educational systems has increased the scope of professional opportunities for females. At the same time, boys and adult males tend to be more aggressive and assertive and to commit more homicides than girls and women, as also holds true in preindustrial societies. While gender equality is increasingly considered an official ideal in modern societies, males continue to dominate the political system, especially in East Asia. Neolocal residence has become predominant, especially in the individualistic Western societies, where it tends to weaken the power and cohesion of traditional family systems. This is reflected in high rates of cohabitation, divorce, and singledom in Europe and North America, practices that can have negative consequences for children (Klinenberg, 2013).

In general, the accelerating forces that are driving technological and social evolution have exerted an enormous influence on the sheer number of the world's adults and children, together with the lives they lead. For instance, on the eve of the agricultural revolutions, some 10,000 to 13,000 years ago, a mere 4–8 million foragers roamed the earth in mostly small groups (Roser & Ortiz-Ospina, 2018a). This may be compared to today's global population of 7.6 billion that includes 2.3 billion children below the age of eighteen. Thus, in terms of numbers, humanity probably increased during these years by a factor of at least 1,000.

We have selected four specific sociocultural groups for our comparisons because they exemplify four types of subsistence economy, are dynamic in nature, differ in the nature of their children's day-to-day lives, and yet have not been previously compared by cross-cultural psychologists. Varying enormously in size, complexity, access to technologies, and political influence, they all have interacted in the course of history with neighboring and/or occupying societies. Three of the four cultural groups, namely the Australian Aborigines, Tibetan nomads, and Maya peasants, were incorporated into more powerful societies through conquest and thereby acquired minority group status. In addition and like other sociocultural groups, they are increasingly gaining access to more than one form of subsistence technology and consequently are undergoing accelerating changes, especially in recent times. These changes are having numerous positive and negative repercussions for the lives of children and therefore represent an important topic in the later discussions.

Our account of the changing nature of global childhood relies on a variety of methodological approaches. They include those that emphasize participant and behavioral observations together with the delineation of the broader sociocultural context within which children's lives evolve. Such an approach is especially favored by cultural and psychological anthropologists. Anthropologists have also created the basis for systematic comparisons across preindustrial societies by developing major collections of ethnographies, such as those sponsored by Human Relations Area Files (HRAF) (Ember & Ringen, 2017). Also taken into account here is Barry, Child, and Bacon's (1959) pioneering study linking a variety of subsistence economies to child training across 104 preindustrial and mostly nonliterate societies. In addition, we make use of the extensive global data that are being published each year by Roser (2018c), UNICEF, the World Bank, and other sources. Such a multi-method and multidisciplinary approach is well suited for gaining a better understanding of a broad variety of children's lives as they evolve over time. For reasons of space, this publication does not assess important differences in childrearing that exist between the many societies included *within* each of the four categories (e.g., various foraging groups in Australia and elsewhere). Rather, our intent is to delineate in some detail the ecological and sociocultural context of children's lives in four specific societies, and then to arrive at some broader conclusions about the nature of selected global changes in the lives of the world's 2.3 billion children. To do so, we begin by examining Australian Aborigines because they exemplify an ancient but changing and endangered way of life.

2.2 The Children of Australian Aborigines: Then and Now

Homo sapiens is thought to have evolved in Africa some 320,000 to 200,000 years ago and to have arrived in Australia perhaps 60,000 to 65,000 years ago (Reich, 2018). Originally, all members of our species are believed to have lived in hunter-gatherer groups of varying sizes. Indeed, for most of their existence, humans and their hominid predecessors were led by biosocial evolution to adapt to this form of life rather than to live in the much more recent agricultural, pastoral, and postindustrial societies. Keeping such considerations in mind, several studies were initiated in the 1960s, 1970s, and 1980s. Their aim was to understand the lives of children and their elders in selected modern foraging groups such as the Ju/'Hoansi (also called !Kung) of southern Africa's Kalahari Desert (see Lee, 2012), the Aka (Pygmies) of the Congo Basin (Hewlett, 2014), and the Anbarra of northern Australia (Hamilton, 1981). When studying the lifestyles prevailing in these small groups, the researchers were also hoping to throw some tentative light on how our distant ancestors might have lived and behaved – especially after comparing their observations with selected archaeological findings (Zeller, 1987). At the same time, quite a few surprises emerged once anthropologists began to investigate socialization practices and the lives of children among hunter-gatherers such as the Anbarra.

When in 1788 the first groups of British convicts began to settle in the southeastern area of Australia, an estimated 300,000 to 1,000,000 Aborigines were spread across the continent while pursuing a lifestyle based on hunting, gathering, and sometimes fishing. Speaking an estimated 250 to 300 different languages, they lived in smallish separate groups and presumably had pursued their overall way of life for a very long time while having very limited contact with the rest of the world (Broome, 2010). Not surprisingly, various social scientists and Aborigines like to claim that they represent the world's oldest, more or less continuous group of cultures. Thus, Australian Aborigines may be more representative of evolved foraging societies than holds true for some of the more egalitarian groups of African foragers (Hewlett & Lamb, 2005) that for hundreds of years have coexisted with, and often been marginalized by, agriculturalists and pastoralists.

In the years following 1788, many Aborigines experienced Anglo-Saxon colonialism and racism in their most destructive forms. Looked upon as "savages," they often died of diseases they contracted from whites (Hernández, 1941), were killed outright, lost much of their land to the colonizers, suffered from cultural dislocation, and for many years were not entitled to vote. By 1930, their numbers had dwindled to an estimated 50,000 and many Euro-Australians believed that they would soon die out. Especially between the years 1905 and 1969, tens of thousands of biracial or so-called half-caste children were taken away from their Aboriginal mothers and communities. In an effort to obliterate the impact of their native cultures, they were brought up and "saved" in European communities where they attended schools frequently run by Christian church groups. Native memories about these "Stolen Generations" are understandably bitter and constitute one of the many reasons why many indigenous Australians remain skeptical about the motives and goals underlying the laws and institutions aimed at them by Australia's federal and state governments.

Today, Aborigines make up 2.8% of the country's overall population of some 25 million people and their numbers are increasing. While 21% of them live in remote areas, more than a quarter of them reside in big cities, have abandoned their foraging lifestyles, and speak some form of English such as Kriol. In the thinly populated Northern Territories, "homelands" such as Arnhem have been created and many of the region's more than 17,000 indigenous persons live there in various coastal and desert regions. Altogether, they now make up some

30% of all inhabitants in that federal territory and, in 2015, they formed 43% of the territory's youth aged ten to twenty-nine years, given that the average age of indigenous persons is lower than that of the overall population (Institute for Economics and Peace, 2016). Moreover, back in the 1960s, local groups such as the Anbarra ("River Mouth People") were still bringing up their children in mostly traditional ways although they had recently been made to settle down in the small town of Maningrida.

Based on Hamilton's (1981) research as conducted in 1968–1969, Table 2.2 depicts various stages of human development according to the Anbarra people. Prior to conception, a child's spirit is thought to reside in the timeless and sacred era of "Dreaming" when ancestral spirit beings formed the creation. The concept of Dreaming connects Aboriginal societies to a specific land whose custodian they consider themselves to be. At the same time, Dreaming embodies the Law that they must follow. Traditionally, everyday life is suffused with religious interpretations that connect a person to others, life and death, a group's ancestors, the flow of time, the purposes underlying human existence, and nature and "super-nature." Older children and youths slowly learn about the mysterious nature of Dreaming through stories told by their elders at campfires, dancing and chanting, and paintings and figures inscribed in the sand and on bark. Moreover, secret, gender-specific, and drawn-out initiation rites are of great importance for the lives of boys and, in a good many Aboriginal societies, for girls and women as well (Hamilton, 1980).

When an invisible spirit-child decides to be born, it may crawl up the legs of its future mother and enter her womb or else it may hide in a fish or other aquatic creature it somehow knows will soon be eaten by its future mother. More generally, humans are believed to emerge from the Dreaming, return to their ancestors at the time of their death, and probably seek rebirth at some future time. After a child is born, it is frequently breastfed for several years and cuddled quite a bit. Young children are considered "women's business" while typical fathers are warm and supportive, but a bit distant. Infants and toddlers co-sleep with their mother or, at times, with some other adult(s) such as their grandma. As in other Aboriginal societies, it is the child who decides when it is to be breastfed, when it is ready to take a nap, and when it wants to sit on his or her mother's shoulders to see more of the world around it. In this way, it is granted considerable autonomy while receiving few specific instructions. "The assumption is that whatever the child wants is what it needs" (Hamilton, 1981, p. 128). At the same time, the child, from early on, will be encouraged to share food and other desirable goods, especially with younger children. Thus, the child is taught to be nurturing and generous and to avoid selfishness. Older

Table 2.2 Stages of Development among the Anbarra (1968–1969)

Before conception	The invisible spirit child resides in the timeless "Dreaming"; humans emerge from it and return to it after death
Conception	A spirit child "catches" his/her future mother
Birth	Inside; the tiny one
Three to six weeks (diffuse attachment)	The smile; the boy, the girl
Six months (intense attachment to mother)	Sitting up: he who sits on the shoulder
Eighteen to twenty-four months (leaving mother's body and breast – hates mother)	Giving up mother, the frightened one
Three years (joins peer group in camp) (may still be breastfed)	The cheeky one (permissive childrearing)
Five years (leaves camp group to join other children)	The "kid mob"
Nine to twelve years (prepuberty)	Boys: "the big ones"
Boys move to bachelors' camp for a series of secret initiation rituals and instructions; girls join their (older) husbands to whom they were promised early on	Girls: "the breasts"
Women: First child at 15.9 years	*Gama*
Older men: Dominate the culture	*Wura* (some older men have two or three wives)
Death ("Sorry time": certain rituals must be performed)	Spirit returns to the "Dreaming Time Ancestors" and is likely to be reborn; no clear conception of heaven or hell

Source: Annette Hamilton (1981). *Nature and Nurture: Aboriginal Child Rearing in North-Central Arnhem Land.* Canberra, Australia: Australian Institute of Aboriginal Studies.

people's messages to that effect are often indirect in nature and should the young child choose not to obey them, it will probably not be criticized in a direct way (see also Hernández's [1941] description of the privileged status of children among the Drysdale River tribes). Surrounded by classificatory "mothers" (including the mother's sisters), the matrilineal grandmother, and other children, the child is granted considerable autonomy from early on but at the same time remains embedded in a shifting group of adults and children. The emerging self-conceptions of the child are, step by step, "anchored in kin relationships" (Eickelkamp, 2011a, p. 135). Little privacy or isolation exists for the young child, and it is unlikely to be physically punished or harshly criticized.

Beginning around the age of three, the child joins its peer group of boys and girls in its camp. Around five or six years of age, he or she begins to segregate more continuously according to sex and to explore the environment near the camp. In this context, children in general, and above all the boys, enjoy a considerable degree of autonomy and engage in playful activities that are mostly unsupervised by adults. In their excursions, groups of boys may try to catch small animals such as lizards weighing a few pounds. Girls may be asked to take care of younger kids, but they can also be seen to gather food reasonably close to the camps. Some boys and girls will also explore each other's bodies in playful ways.

Many Aboriginal societies such as the Anbarra are (or were) mostly controlled by elderly men who strategically claim to be in possession of secret knowledge about the mythic beings of Dreaming. These beings, in turn, are thought to have established the local social order that incorporates elaborate kinship systems, age categories, and unequal gender roles. This secret knowledge is conveyed to nine-to-twelve-year-old boys in bachelors' camps via detailed instructions and a series of initiation rituals. (For an account of women's secret rites in a different Aboriginal society, see Hamilton, 1980.) By way of contrast, many young girls around the time of their menarche, or even earlier, join their much older husbands, to whom they had been promised at an early age. Such marriages are based on a series of complex negotiations and marriage promises designed to establish linkages between families and clans. In contrast, the feelings of the marriage partners for each other are considered less important. Sexual relations between the young wives and their husbands might begin before puberty and frequently result in early pregnancies. Ideally, men have more than one wife, in part because they enjoy sexual variety and in part because it helps them to control the fates of many children and thereby increase their status and power. Physical violence by husbands, and sometimes by brothers, against younger women and girls does sometimes occur and may lead to serious injuries. Such violence can also result in potentially destructive quarrels within and between extended families and clans.

Since Hamilton conducted her research, many changes have occurred in the lives of Australian Aborigines. They have disproportionately increased in number and the Australian government apologized to them in 2008 for the policies and events surrounding the Stolen Generations. More schools and health care facilities have been built for them, and their overall situation has been the subject of various government reports, research studies (Penman, 2006), and frequent media coverage. Moreover, indigenous artists have become well known for their ability to convey selected aspects of their spiritual traditions through paintings, sculptures, music, and dancing to both cultural insiders and outsiders. At the same time, however, Aborigines remain the most troubled ethnic-racial group in Australian society.

In 2016, the Australian government published a report comparing Australian youth development in different states and groups based on the internationally developed Youth Development Index (YDI). The Australian YDI represents a composite index of sixteen indicators assessing the five domains of education, health and well-being, employment, political participation, and civic participation of ten-to-twenty-nine-year-old youth across the nation's eight states and territories. The index ranges from a low score of 0 to a perfect score of 1 and resembles the United Nations' Human Development Index (HDI) (Institute for Economics and Peace, 2016).

Seen internationally, Australia's impressive 2016 YDI of 0.84 ranks third highest among 185 nations and easily surpasses the global average of 0.66. However, the score varies dramatically between the country's states and territories and ranges from a dismal score of 0.294 in the New Territories (43% of its youth come from an indigenous background) to a very high score of 0.851 in the Australian Capital Territory (less than 3% of its youth are indigenous). The indigenous younger youth tend to score low in regard to indicators of literacy, numeracy, and school attendance. At the same time, the older youth are much more likely to be unemployed compared to other groups. Indigenous youth living in the cities are more likely to do well academically than their peers residing in the more remote regions of the New Territories and western Australia. Perhaps this is so in part because the indigenous city youth are surrounded by Australians of mostly European and Asian backgrounds that are psychologically invested in their education and enjoy the support of middle-class parents. Moreover, well-educated Aboriginal men and women in the larger east coast cities are far more likely to be married to nonindigenous spouses than those living in the outback areas (O'Loughlin, 2009).

Indigenous male youth between twenty-five and twenty-nine years have some of the highest suicide rates in the world (Institute for Economics and

Peace, 2016). Altogether, the average life expectancy of indigenous persons is a striking twenty years lower than that for the total Australian overall population (Penman, 2006, p. 2). To add to this bleak picture, cross-cultural comparisons suggest that Australia's indigenous people tend to be psychologically even worse off than the rather troubled indigenous inhabitants of New Zealand, Canada, and the United States, with whom they may be fruitfully compared given their fairly similar colonial histories (Buti, 2002).

In recent decades, rapid sociocultural and ecological changes have influenced the lives and self-conceptions of the children and adolescents growing up in Australia's indigenous communities (Eickelkamp, 2011b). Some youthful members may try some combination of foraging, wage labor, creating and selling art, going to school, and serving as a tourist guide. Especially in the remote areas, families may go on social welfare while relying less exclusively on their former ways of hunting and gathering. On the basis of what they learn in their schools and what they see and hear through videos, rap music, the Web, and TV shows, the older children in particular are exposed to novel and potentially seductive aspects of Australian and Western mainstream cultures that frequently are at odds with their own cultural traditions (Malin, Campbell, & Agius, 1996). In consequence, traditional religious ideas about Dreaming and the Law as well as communal childrearing responsibilities may prove less convincing to the younger generations. This, in turn, is bound to undermine the authority of their elders. Young teenage girls, for instance, increasingly refuse to marry their assigned older husbands-to-be, engage in sex with younger and perhaps unemployed men, sometimes contract sexually transmitted diseases such as chlamydia, and may get pregnant. In the latter case, they tend to drop out of school (at least initially) and may become restless mothers in spite of their family's positive response to their new child. A considerable number of today's Aboriginal families are matriarchal and held together by women.

A disproportionate percentage of male teenagers, in turn, drop out of school and lack clear plans for their future. Instead, they may play cards, gamble, get addicted to alcohol, begin sniffing petrol, and get involved in fights (Atkinson, 2009). A highly disproportionate percentage of them end up in detention centers, where they are often severely abused by guards (Australian Institute of Family Studies, 2017; Royal Commission and Board of Inquiry into Protection and Detention Systems of the Northern Territories, 2017). In today's context of potentially fragmented sociocultural identities and eroding support for self-regulatory values, male and sometimes female alcoholism and drug abuse can result in a transgenerational chain reaction revolving around family, disorientation and anomie, violence, unemployment, self-destruction, and sexual abuse of girls. It is also clear that the traditional roles of men as hunters, providers, protectors, and leaders are eroding and that many teenagers find it difficult to prosper in what they regard as a white man's world.

In response to these troublesome developments, native representatives, as well as government agencies and sympathetic social scientists, sometimes underline the positive characteristics of native communities. For instance, they like to discuss permissive childrearing styles that aim to encourage both the children's autonomy and their social responsiveness (e.g., Secretariat of National Aboriginal and Torres Strait Islander Child Care, 2011). It remains unclear, however, whether this form of childrearing prepares children to prosper in modern schools based on clear authority structures, as exemplified by the demanding South Korean educational system discussed later on. Doing well in quality schools requires determination, the ability to defer gratification, a long-term perspective, and high degrees of self-control that students need to develop from early on, together with the knowledgeable support of somewhat "pushy" parents. In contrast, when children from Aboriginal families enter the school system, they often experience culture shock given the discrepancies between their permissive childrearing and the structured demands of the school system, which tends to be exacerbated by experiences of prejudice coming from some of the other children.

Some critics blame problems in the indigenous communities almost exclusively on white racism (e.g., McGlade, 2012), even though misogynist violence and sexual abuse of girls already existed in various indigenous communities in precontact times (Jarrett, 2013). In addition, such problems can be seen in a number of today's (more or less) self-determined communities in the Northern Territories and elsewhere. Still, it is understandable that community organizers are drawn to a strength-based approach since successful social intervention programs should appeal to the members of native communities and incorporate their positive sociocultural characteristics. In addition, indigenous representatives increasingly insist that they must be consulted when outsiders conduct research in their respective societies. However, male representatives of the Aboriginal community may not always adequately represent the overall situation and interests of female teenagers and women. Altogether, it is clear that the integration of many indigenous youth, children, and cultural groups into Australian society has encountered serious obstacles (Newton, 2017). In consequence, finding better forms of bicultural integration will pose a difficult task in the years ahead for both the communities themselves as well as society at large.

2.3 Growing Up among Tibetan Herdsmen, Yaks, Lamas, and Bandits

Covering about 970,000 square miles, the Tibetan High Plateau or "Roof of the World" is the world's highest and most extensive plateau. Many of its areas are situated at average heights of 14,000 to 17,500 feet that are mostly unsuitable for agriculture. Located predominantly in western and southwestern China, with small southern extensions reaching into the Ladakh region of northwestern India, western Nepal, and Bhutan, the often treeless northern grasslands have, for at least 4,000 years, formed the home of hardy *drokpa* ("high-pasture people"). These Tibetan nomads depend on herds of yak, sheep, goats, and some horses for their livelihood (Miller, 2007). In contrast, agriculturalists can be found in many of the plateau's lower-lying and southern areas. During the long and brutal winter months, temperatures in the northern highlands frequently drop to −40 to −20 degrees Fahrenheit, yet the nomads' animals need to graze regardless of such temperatures. In addition, they must be protected against wolves, bears, and snow leopards. Fierce hail and snow storms sometimes injure or kill whole groups of animals while others may be stolen by rival nomads. Herding on the roof of the world carries with it many risks. Thus, whenever possible, the nomads will move their tents and herds to lower-lying areas during the long winter months, but even then daily life is likely to be demanding. In addition, the nomads like to trade with farmers and town dwellers and celebrate their physical skills by participating in, and attending, popular horse races and wrestling contests.

Traditionally, the Tibetans distinguished between the western areas of Ü-Thant (now mostly incorporated into the Tibetan Autonomous Region) and the eastern areas of Amdo (predominantly in the Qinghai Province) and Kham (mostly in Sichuan and the Tibetan Autonomous Region). During the first five decades of the twentieth century, Ü-Thant functioned largely as an independent country, whose theocratic and largely feudal government tried as much as possible to isolate the country from the rest of the world in order to better protect its factual independence, feudal social structure, and religious institutions. This was one of the reasons why not a single road crossed an area as large as Western Europe. In contrast, fierce fighting sometimes erupted in Amdo and Kham between Chinese Hui (Muslims) and Tibetan nomads. At the same time, nomads in the latter areas were politically independent from the theocratic Tibetan government in Lhasa. Still, they tended to recognize Lhasa as their most important religious center and the Dalai Lama as the central religious authority of their Buddhist religion. Indeed, the fourteenth Dalai Lama (*1935) was born in Taktser, a small village located in Amdo. After his early identification as the reincarnation of the recently deceased thirteenth Dalai Lama, he was brought to Lhasa as a child.

These political developments came to an end in the 1950s, when China's new Communist regime first invaded Tibet and some years later defeated a popular uprising that originally had started among nomads and monks residing in the Kham and Amdo regions. The rebellion soon spread to the Tibetan Autonomous Region and resulted in widespread killings and the destruction of numerous Buddhist monasteries by the Chinese troops (Lehmann & Ullal, 1981; see also Nulo, 2014, for a child's perspective on these upheavals). When its impact began to weaken in 1959, the Dalai Lama escaped to India. There he and the present Tibetan government in exile reside until this day.

The traditional nomadic lifestyle was alive and well during the late 1930s and 1940s when German Tibetologist and Christian missionary Matthias Hermanns explored the family life of Amdo Pa (or people of Amdo) in the Kokonor Lake region (Hermanns, 1959). Speaking one of the Amdo dialects as well as Chinese, Hermanns had also received medical training. This, in turn, facilitated his access to women and children as well as men. In this context, Hermanns described a special form of "nomad psychology" that in his view is shaped by the extremely demanding ecological conditions to which the tent dwellers must adapt. The nomads are forced to follow the rhythms of nature in order to control them – or else risk disaster. Trying to survive, males in particular need to be physically strong, steadfast, mobile, and able to endure extreme physical conditions. They should have excellent vision so they can identify animals and people at long distances, be able to hear and distinguish between numerous and often subtle sounds that could indicate potential opportunities or dangers, remain consistently vigilant against human and nonhuman predators, and be capable of calmly planning ahead while keeping tight rein over their fears and impulses. Assertive and courageous, the nomads are often imperious while disdaining any signs of weakness or cowardice both in others and in themselves. They possess a clear sense of autonomy, yet at the same time they must be able to cooperate with family and tribal members. Otherwise, they and their family will sooner or later fail to prosper. Many nomads love to hunt although their Buddhist convictions tell them that killing animals will worsen their individual *karma* and consequently the form their reincarnation will assume. To win a horse race or a wrestling match brings much honor to a young man – and hopefully a not-so-chaste tryst with an admiring and adventuresome maiden. Tibetan nomads love to sing, dance, and hear tales of valor such as the famous Gesar Epos, but they also respond positively to famous *rinpoche* (religious teachers, recognized reincarnations) who not only serve their religious needs but may also be asked to mediate between conflicting clans or tribal groups.

The nomads follow a patrilineal and patrilocal kinship system that strongly emphasizes "bone relationships" along male lines as well as a common ancestor. However, variations in family structures commonly occur depending on a given family's wealth, how many male and female children have survived, individual preferences and dislikes, and potential or real conflicts between various members of the extended family. In many of the large and comfortable tents made from black yak hair, one can find some five to ten persons, including retired grandparents, the oldest son who is in charge of the family, his wife and children, perhaps one or two younger brothers with or without children, and unmarried sisters. Upon marriage, the new wife is expected to move to the tent of her husband, where she comes under the control of her new mother-in-law. In those cases where there is no son, the oldest daughter will marry a *magpa* (often the son of a poor family) who will then move into his wife's tent and over time gain in authority. Some younger daughters may have an illegitimate child or two, but such situations tend to evoke only mild criticism. Indeed, when an important guest stays with the family, a teenage daughter may be asked whether she would be willing to sleep with him. Hermanns claimed that most daughters look forward to such an experience.

On the whole, Tibetan women enjoy a higher status and more freedoms than women in neighboring societies such as (traditional) mainstream China, India, and nowadays Pakistan. For instance, the same names are sometimes used for women and men, such as Pema (Lotus Flower). However, women's status does not equal that of men (Gielen, 1993). While many marriages are arranged among the nomads of Amdo, very few of them practice polygyny unless the wife is infertile. Similarly, fraternal polyandry (a wife is married to two or more brothers) is rare among the Amdo Pa, although it is common among some other Tibetan groups. Tibetan women, however, generally play a limited role in politics, and nuns have a lower status and considerably less influence than the much more numerous and powerful monks.

A popular saying in Amdo states that "a woman unable to have children is frequently ill." As holds true among quite a few other traditional Asian peoples, children are considered of central importance to a couple's happiness together with the benefits of enjoying a long life and having access to sufficient economic resources. If a future wife gives birth to a child prior to getting married, this may not be considered a major problem since, after all, it proves her fertility. Abortions are only very rarely performed. Childless couples, in turn, will consult with a holy lama and probably be told by him to go on a long pilgrimage and to prostrate themselves numerous times while circumambulating a famous monastery such as Kumbum.

Nomadic women in Amdo tend to have somewhat lower birth rates than the women of farmers, in part because living at very high altitudes appears to be detrimental to their fertility (Cameron & Bogin, 2012). Moreover, overall child mortality rates at the time of Hermanns's research were apparently very high and may have surpassed 50%. The average age of menarche is about thirteen to fourteen years, child marriages hardly ever occur, and most women have their first child around the ages of eighteen to twenty years. They give birth in a variety of situations, but preferably in a small tent that has been erected for this purpose near the main tent. If available, the grandma or another experienced woman helps the mother-to-be, but a solitary birth may occur when, for instance, she is working in the grasslands. Soon after the child's arrival, the beaming father kisses his newborn and is likely to consult a well-paid astrologer whose elaborate calculations, explanations, predictions, and advice he is likely to take very seriously. Based on the exact date and time of the child's birth, the astrologer suggests a name for him or her, makes predictions about the child's likely lifespan, and suggests defensive religio-magical rituals to better protect the little one against demons, other dangers, and the malevolent glances of envious neighbors. Other parents wait until their child is about one year old and then ask a lama to assign a name to their child. The name should transfer the lama's wisdom to the child and protect it against ill fortune and illnesses caused by angry spirits originating from the "muck of life."

Giving birth to her first child – especially if it is a son who in later years will inherit the tent and the herds of yaks and sheep that go with it – solidifies the position of the young mother in the family. If her husband is an oldest son, she can look forward to a time when she will become the "mistress of the tent," a much-desired position. To the husband, becoming the father of one or more sons means that he will have descendants, continue his family line, and be surrounded by children and grandchildren in his old age.

Young children are breastfed on demand for two to four years. Physical punishment is uncommon at least during their early years and the children tend to be enveloped by an atmosphere of love created by their mother, grandparents, other women, and older siblings. Once they can walk and run, they like to play with little sheep, behave like small dogs, or imitate quite convincingly the birds with which they are familiar. However, they are unlikely to own many toys. Once they are a few years old, the girls in particular will be given some ring(s) and other small jewelry. After all, Tibetan nomads love to dress up for special occasions, and their children like to follow in their elders' footsteps as much as possible.

From early on, children learn about adult responsibilities in a playful yet increasingly demanding way. The girls learn, mostly through observation, how to milk animals and to create butter, make *tsampa* from roasted barley and yak butter, brew different types of tea, collect and dry yak and sheep dung, fetch water, and take care of younger kids. Little age segregation exists. For instance, it is not uncommon for five-year-olds to carry an infant on their back or to see them playing with other kids while watching a toddler. There is little doubt that most girls and women work harder than the boys and men, a pattern that is widespread in preindustrial societies (Larson & Verma, 1999). Young boys and some of the girls learn to take care of young sheep kept near the tent, but by the age of about nine to eleven years, the boys are beginning to guide some of the family's herds of sheep and yaks to their grazing areas. Starting around the age of sixteen, youths begin to kill and slaughter animals. Constructing their own kinds of slingshots and using stones as projectiles, they are able to hit targets such as straying sheep and even threatening wolves from astonishing distances. They learn how to ride horses, endure extreme weather conditions, and entertain themselves by hunting marmosets and hares. In this way, they are becoming, step by step, skillful, hardy, watchful, and courageous nomads. They acquire that special kind of "nomad psychology" that Westerners such as Ekvall (1968), Hermanns (1959), and Miller (2007) have learned to admire and, on occasion, to romanticize.

The Amdo Pa see themselves embedded in a universe that is governed by magical-religious forces and beings. These include numerous spirits inhabiting towering mountains, high passes, the earth, and the at times numinous and at other times sinister sky. Such spirits must be propitiated or else they will exert their revenge. Various forms of Vajrayana Buddhism and/or the indigenous Bön religion are widely accepted by both the nomadic and non-nomadic Amdo Pa and form a central part of their worldview. Not only do groups of nomads support local monasteries economically, but a good number of families will send one of their five-to-seven-year-old sons to join "their" monastery, where he will be brought up as a monk. In particular, parents may ask one of their younger sons whether he wishes to join, and especially so if he appears to have the right temperament and outlook for such an avocation. Monks take their vows around the age of eighteen to twenty years, although some of them leave the monastery during their teenage years or even after they have taken their vows. Moreover, many mothers hope that one of their sons will be recognized as a high-ranking reincarnation, an event that may occur when the son is about three to four years old. To qualify for this recognition, the child is expected to possess certain physical characteristics and to be able to identify various ritual objects that originally belonged to a recently deceased *rinpoche*. Indeed, the boy is believed to share his spiritual essence and "mind-stream" with the *rinpoche* as well as with his predecessors whose name he will adopt and perpetuate. Once officially recognized as the new reincarnation, the boy is taken to "his" monastery, where from childhood on he will be brought up as a future leader. To become the honored mother of such a well-known reincarnation has been the dream of many a Tibetan woman. At the same time, monasteries help to reinforce the communal nature of Tibetan nomadic and semi-nomadic societies (Schneider, 2016).

Since Hermanns conducted his research in the late 1930s and 1940s, Tibetan nomads have been experiencing many positive, negative, and mixed changes (Tan, 2017). Many of them are being brought about by their incorporation into the economic, political, and sociocultural structures mostly created by the Chinese government in faraway Beijing. A central goal of both the central and the local governments is to settle the nomads down and to break their resistance against China's totalitarian and anti-religious form of "socialism with Chinese characteristics," which the traditionally religious and freely roaming nomads tend to oppose. In recent decades, the government has been trying to induce or else force nomads to build houses at various distances from the higher-lying pastures while offering them considerable financial support to do so. Furthermore, the government has been creating large national parks and establishing restricted areas for many nomads while insisting that it is forced to do so in order to protect the high pasture grasslands against destructive overgrazing by the nomads' animals. These assertions have been repeatedly criticized (Isom, 2009).

The formerly very high mortality rates for nomadic children have been declining substantially and consequently their population is increasing. In addition, the Chinese government is demanding that all children go to school – preferably for at least nine years (Postiglione, Jiao, & Goldstein, 2011). In response, many nomadic parents are now sending some or all of their children to a boarding school in a more or less distant town, where they may be initially instructed in Tibetan and, starting with secondary school, in Mandarin (Bangsbo, 2008). Not only do such linguistic policies place the Tibetan children at a distinct educational disadvantage when compared to their Han (ethnic Chinese) peers but they also continue China's centuries-old efforts to promote the Sinification of its non-Han populations. The Sinification policies are intended to strengthen the Tibetan children's identification both with China as their socialist "motherland" and with its dominant Han culture. After all, and for numerous centuries, Han have tended to look down upon Mongolian, Tibetan, and other nomads as backward and potentially dangerous people who need to be civilized and tamed through immersion in what many Han consider to be the foremost and oldest continuous civilization on earth. A good many Chinese thought of the Amdo Pa as "Western barbarians" (Hermanns, 1959, p. 184). These days they may also be considered "younger brothers" who need to be guided by their older, better educated, and wiser Han brothers – whether they like this idea or not. Various traditional Tibetan nomads, in turn, disdain Han (and also Tibetan) farmers and city dwellers because of their seeming lack of true freedom and independence. They also see them as lacking the nomads' physical and mental hardiness and abilities, courage, and unique character. At the same time, given the military superiority of the country's People's Liberation Army, the former and at times extensive fighting between Tibetans and Chinese largely ceased after the early 1960s.

The nomadic children's situation in the often Han-ruled boarding schools brings with it major challenges. Many of them miss the emotional warmth of their families as well as the kind of life that had surrounded them in earlier days in the form of open skies, towering mountains, expansive grasslands, sturdy yaks, swift horses, and self-possessed people exuding a special feeling of freedom. Moreover, they tend to see themselves as outsiders in their schools, often experience academic difficulties when having to compete against Chinese and Tibetan children coming from literate and urban homes, and are at a major disadvantage if and when they need to learn spoken and written Mandarin. For bicultural teenagers trying to reconcile two very different ways of life, cultural beliefs, languages, and political ideologies, forming a stable identity is bound to pose serious problems and create confusion for some of them. At the same time, they are told that they must get a good education and master Chinese if they wish to have any chance for an economically promising future.

However, not all students miss the brutal hardships that accompany nomadic life on the world's frigid "third pole." Instead, they (or some part of them) may feel relieved and privileged, yet just those feelings can also lead to a pronounced psychological gap between themselves and their often illiterate or semiliterate parents, grandparents, and tent-dwelling siblings. The generational transitions, then, between the older nomads or ex-nomads and their school-going and town-dwelling children and grandchildren are liable to create both tensions and opportunities not only for the nomadic Amdo Pa and Kham Pa but also for other nomads such as those residing in the Ladakh region of India (Dollfus, 2013), Mongolia, Inner Mongolia (a province of China), Central Asia, and elsewhere. In Mongolia, for instance, large numbers of nomads are now moving to the country's capital, Ulaanbaatar, because of climate changes, droughts, harsh winters, dying animals, and overgrazing due to rapid population increases. For their children, that means poverty and pressures to do well in school, together with contrary pressures to find a paying job as soon as possible and major changes in lifestyle (Baring, 2018).

2.4 From Subsistence Economy to Cash Economy: Maya Villagers and Townspeople

The modern Maya are the largest Mesoamerican Indian group inhabiting parts of southern Mexico, Guatemala, Belize, El Salvador, and Honduras. Composed of approximately 7–7.5 million people, they speak some thirty languages, many of which are mutually unintelligible. In addition, they tend to speak Spanish with the *Ladinos*, Westernized persons of mixed Spanish and indigenous descent. Many *Ladinos* live in towns, are members of the middle and working classes, and not rarely look down on the Maya as unsophisticated indigenous peasants. This situation derives from colonial history as well as the fact that many Maya are agriculturalists and live in villages, farm homesteads, and small towns. Using hoes and digging sticks, they raise corn, beans, and squash. In addition, they may keep animals such as pigs, goats, chickens, ducks, and turkeys. Their women often wear beautiful and self-made traditional dresses, whereas most men prefer modern ready-made clothes. Modern Maya increasingly live in a changing and multicultural world in which Maya, Hispanic, general Mexican, Guatemalan or Belizean, Catholic, Evangelical-Protestant, and US-American cultural strands have increasingly become intertwined.

The Maya are the inheritors of one of Mesoamerica's leading ancient cultures that was literate, developed sophisticated mathematical and astronomical systems, and created impressive temples and towering pyramids. For some not fully understood reasons, a major part of the Mayan civilization collapsed around 850 CE–900 CE. Following the Spanish conquest in the sixteenth century, the Maya dwindled in numbers and were forced into brutish servitude. Coerced to adopt Catholicism as their religion, they tacitly incorporated many indigenous and unorthodox features into their Catholic practices. While today's Catholic Maya participate in many saints' feast days, various Protestant and often US-American missionaries and groups such as Evangelicals and Pentecostals have, in recent decades, made considerable inroads among them. Protestant groups downplay the importance of saints, emphasize the study of the Bible, and are said be relatively successful in the fight against men's alcoholism that can undermine the welfare of families. Other Maya are rejecting Christian worship in favor of ancestral rites. In addition, many Guatemalan families are still recovering from the country's genocidal civil war (1960–1996), which led to an estimated 200,000 killings and widespread human rights abuses by the US-supported army and government against Maya and other farmers and workers (Schlesinger, Kinzer, & Coatsworth, 2005). Although many Maya migrated to the United States and elsewhere during and after the civil war, they nevertheless continue to make up about 39–41% of the Guatemalan population. Others live in many parts of Mexico's Yucatan Peninsula.

In 2005, Karen L. Kramer published a book based on her fieldwork in the small and isolated Maya village of Xculoc in Yucatan. Based on research conducted in 1992–1993, 2001, and 2003, the book attempts to answer the questions why and how the poor subsistence farmers of Xculoc successfully raised large numbers of children. In this context, the author noted that "even though from a young age children spent long hours working, parents did not have enough time in the day to support their families" (p. 1). Kramer's central question is one that may be asked about many other poor but fertile peasant societies.

At the time of Kramer's initial study in 1992–1993, Xculoc, with its 316 inhabitants, had no access to electricity or running water. Neither did the village include a clinic, although health care providers would periodically visit it to vaccinate the children. When children became seriously ill, villagers had to take them to the next town to see a doctor or pharmacist. Nevertheless, child mortality among Maya peasants had already declined dramatically from its earlier, far higher levels (cf. Gaskins, 2003); indeed, some 95% of all children in Xculoc survived to age fifteen. In general, the villagers were adequately nourished and appeared in good health. School-aged children were sent to the local primary school even though teachers would not always show up for their job. Still, most children learned to read and write in Spanish although they rarely received higher education in one of the nearby towns. Between them, the villagers used Yucatec Mayan as their major language and many members of the elder generation understood little, if any, Spanish.

Most couples were locals and got married early. Their marital relationships tended to be amiable, none of their marriages had ended in divorce, and none of the children were considered illegitimate. The prevailing gender roles followed a general pattern that can also be found in many other villages around the world. Thus, the women and their daughters were heavily involved in domestic activities such as food processing, cooking tortillas and other forms of food preparation, collecting firewood and water, tending a variety of domesticated animals, sewing and embroidering, washing, and cleaning. In addition, the daughters from early on were responsible for taking care of younger siblings. With the exception of cutting firewood in the forest, most of these activities took place in the village. By comparison, the men and older boys performed field and garden work that took them outside the village. Their physically demanding work included preparing new forest plots as well as weeding previously used plots. This meant felling trees, field burning, seed preparation, planting, crop maintenance, and harvesting. They also transported goods between the village and the *milpas* (maize fields). In addition, some men taught their sons more risky and forest-related activities such as hunting. In general, the traditional culture incorporated many collectivistic beliefs that helped to create cultural cohesion among family members and more generally among the villagers. Accordingly, the children learned from the older generations and their older siblings what was expected of them within the context of their daily activities. Already by the age of two, many Maya children keenly observed and attempted to actively participate in adult work (Martinéz-Pérez, 2015). Experiencing little age segregation, they spent most of their time interacting with members of their extended family. This pattern has also been found in other studies of Maya children (Gaskins, 2000, 2006; Maynard 2002).

Mothers had their first baby at an average age of 19.5. The families greatly valued having many children, and thus the average family included about seven of them. From early on, the children contributed their work to the welfare of their families and became "helpers at the farm" (the telling subtitle of Kramer's book). For instance, young girls assisted as well as they could in the lengthy, complicated, and crucial task of maize processing and undertook other domestic work. As they were growing older, they learned to prepare food, sew and embroider, wash and hang up clothes, scrub floors, and occasionally feed fowl and pigs. Girls merely a few years old were already responsible for taking care of their still younger siblings and over time learned how to guide them (Maynard, 2002). Just a bit later, they began to contribute to field work in addition to their domestic work. Beginning around the age of about two and a half to three years, both girls and boys were sent out on small errands in a village where just about everybody would know them and, if necessary, keep an eye on them. Thus, the villagers were much more involved in each other's lives than is typically found in modern cities – whether that be Cancún, Mexico City, Seoul, or Sydney. By the age of about seven years, the boys would accompany their fathers to the fields. There, they participated in preparing fields, planting and harvesting maize, and taking care of various other plants. Importantly and based on Kramer's carefully collected data, children began to "earn their keep" in their later teenage years. In other words, they began to produce more than they consumed. This must have contributed to their usefulness and consequently to the prevailing large family sizes. In contrast to this situation, only a few teenagers earn their keep in modern information societies.

Ten years later, the world of these villagers had already changed substantially. Supported by a better road system, improved water lines, the village's first electrical lines, and the arrival of a junior high school, both children and adults had become more aware of the outside world. The children in particular were beginning to watch TV while others continued to attend school during their early to middle teenage years. School attendance, however, began to undermine some of the children's practical skills and their contributions as "helpers of the farm." Some girls, for instance, became less proficient as weavers and embroiderers. And when a hurricane in 2002 destroyed most of the crops, many men and (for the first time) some young women began to work in a nearby town at least on a temporary basis. Moreover, the rapid expansion of the population was beginning to lead to deforestation, an undersupply of fields, more inequality, and more pressure on the men to earn some of their income elsewhere.

More recently, and based on various other studies, a good number of young men have been leaving their Maya villages in order to assume jobs in the expanding tourist industry or some local factory in places such as Cancún and the Caribbean coast (Goldin, 2011). There they are more likely to be successful if they speak Spanish reasonably well. Others prefer to return to their villages as soon as possible in order to enjoy their family lives and because of their negative encounters with some *Ladinos* (Gaskins, 2003).

Whereas Kramer's initial study took us to a small, isolated Mexican village in the early 1990s, Barbara Rogoff's (2011) work centers on the long life of a sacred Maya midwife working in San Pedro la Laguna, an expanding Guatemalan town overlooking beautiful Lake Atitlán. Her book is about spiritual inspiration and destiny, ancient birthing practices, mothers together with their babies and children, the rapid transformation of cultural practices, the introduction of schooling mostly in Spanish rather than the local Tz'utujil Mayan language, declining child mortality and birth rates, people who gossip until they are interrupted by cellphone calls, and the university-educated grandchildren of an illiterate yet much admired midwife.

In 1925, when future midwife Encarnación Chona Pérez was born, San Pedro had around 2,000 predominantly Maya inhabitants. When Kramer began her research in 1974, San Pedro's population had increased to approximately 5,000. Today, the beautifully situated town is home to a good 13,000 people. They include a fair number of American and European expatriates and backpackers. While only some Maya children attended school in the old days, today just about all of them are enrolled – and many complete all twelve grades and perhaps even tertiary education. Indeed, San Pedro nowadays exports quite a few well-educated teachers to the rest of Guatemala.

Potential Maya midwives such as Chona are born with the birth sign that indicates their special avocation and destiny, although quite a few chosen ones will later settle on another and less demanding profession. Other midwives-to-be resist their destiny but after becoming ill, they reconsider and enter the path they believe was meant for them. To become a midwife represents a spiritual calling, an obstetric profession, and a much-honored position. By 2010, Chona had assisted in the birth of roughly one-half of all *Pedranos* (inhabitants of San Pedro). Moreover, given the prevailing very high infant and mother mortality rates, especially prior to the 1980s to 1990s, a midwife's skills or lack of skills could mean the difference between life and death. It is no surprise, then, that when Chona walks through the town's streets, many locals will respectfully kiss the back of her hand. Is she not their symbolic mother or grandmother?

Like many of her peers, Chona got already married at age fifteen, and gave birth to the first of her ten children at age sixteen. However, only four of the ten survived, with most of the others being killed by measles. In many other families as well, whooping cough, diarrhea, and measles killed at least half of their children during the 1930s and 1940s. Today, however, child mortality rates have declined sharply, as they have in so many other countries.

It is both sad and ironic to contemplate that a nationally honored midwife and health expert was unable to save the lives of so many of her own children as well as the lives of a good number of newborns and some of their mothers. Many Maya believe that questions about the life and death of children and adults can be enigmatic and difficult to answer because human destinies so often reflect the impact of supernatural forces and beings. Comparable to traditional Tibetan peasants and nomads, many Maya see themselves surrounded by a broad array of positive as well as dangerous invisible powers that they sometimes attempt to oppose with the help of religio-magical means. Because midwives, like the local shamans, are known for their supernatural journeys, inspirations, and dream-like visions, anxious mothers frequently ask them to treat a young child for "evil eye" and other illnesses. Protestant Maya, however, are less likely to endorse such beliefs since Protestantism represents a form of imported religious modernity within the traditional Mesoamerican context.

In more recent years, the births and lives of children in San Pedro have changed considerably. Although various midwives continue to practice, they are now expected to acquire additional medical knowledge from nurses and doctors at the public health center. However, many doctors are opposed to the traditional practices of midwives and native healers (Cosminsky, 2016). After all, they are convinced that modern vaccination programs and other modern health care practices rather than adherence to traditional procedures are the key to today's sharply lowered mortality rates for infants and young children. In addition, a few *Casas Maternas* (birthing facilities) have been established in Guatemala's highlands (Stollak, Valdez, Rivas, & Perry, 2016). They support traditional birth practices but also offer modern medical services in emergency situations.

Guatemala's TFR was 6.9 children in 1960, but by 2017, it had declined to 2.77. Given a much smaller number of siblings and their long-term school attendance, children are nowadays less extensively involved in sibling care and in helping their parents on a continuous basis. In spite of this, Maya children are more likely than American middle-class children to take on responsibilities at a young age and to learn by pitching in within the context of ongoing family activities. They have also been shown to be better observers while acquiring information and ways of doing things almost by osmosis (Correa-Chávez & Rogoff, 2009; Rogoff, 2011, pp. 248–264). In addition, they pick up knowledge and begin to internalize Maya values by listening to the many stories, tales, and local gossip they hear at home.

Although a good number of *Pedranos* continue as farmers, they are nowadays producing not only for their families but often also for the local, national, and sometimes international markets. Quite a few of their children, in turn, will probably not follow in their parents' footsteps but instead contemplate a range of potential occupations depending on their interests and how successful they are in school. They are exposed to US-American and other Western cultures not only by watching news, sports, and dramas on TV, but also by encountering the many tourists who visit San Pedro and Lake Atitlán. Still others have relatives who have migrated to the United States, send remittances back home, and add a flavor of transnationalism to some children's lives in San Pedro. However, poverty remains widespread, the country's very high crime levels include homicide, rape, and child trafficking, narcotics dealers are powerful, and some husbands end up getting drunk in the numerous local bars. Nevertheless, the experiences, opportunities, and lives of children in San Pedro have become much more varied than those known to previous generations. The opportunities for school-going girls in particular have changed considerably, and a number of them are aiming to become professionals in their future. How different such ambitions are when compared to the lives of traditional mothers just a few decades ago in the small village of Xculoc!

2.5 South Korean Education Fever

In recent decades, a variety of postindustrial information societies have been evolving in North America, Europe, the Middle East, and East Asia. Among these societies, the economic rise of "Confucian Heritage Societies" such as South Korea has been especially rapid. Considering the country's difficult history in the twentieth century, the development of South Korea's information technology industry and culture seems close to miraculous. In 1963, ten years after an armistice ended the Korean War, its gross national income (GNI) per capita was a miniscule $104. Over the course of the next fifty-four years, the same GNI index per capita increased by a factor of 286 and reached $29,745 in 2017 (Bank of Korea, 2018). Today, South Korea is one of the countries where an information technology–related infrastructure and a corresponding lifestyle are most prevalent. According to *The Global Information Technology Report 2016* (World Economic Forum & INSEAD, 2016), South Korea is ranked fifth among countries having the fastest and safest networking capacity and fourth regarding the usage of readily available online services such as banking, buying and selling, entertainment, and education. In addition, it is ranked the world's leading country in that 98.5% of its households can access the Internet while making use of social networking contexts related to public life and to decision-making processes such as a mobile voting system. In general, South Korea has "one of the most tech-savvy populations in the world" (World Economic Forum & INSEAD, 2016).

Many observers consider the "education fever" of South Koreans to be the primary driving force behind this extremely rapid development, which is sometimes called the "Miracle of the Han River" (Seth, 2002). Indeed, academic excellence has been the preeminent value that everyone respects and it is one that South Koreans have been pursuing for centuries. For instance, the Chosun Dynasty (1392~1910 CE) distinguished between four classes of people, namely scholars, farmers, artisans, and tradespeople, and they were respected in that order. Although some of this hierarchical social structure has changed over time, today those scholars who earn higher academic degrees and who appear highly knowledgeable about a given field are still occupying the top rank in people's minds (Seth, 2010).

Based on these cultural and historical considerations, it is natural for us to assume that South Korean parents have as one of their top priorities the academic competence of their children. Then, compared to other civilizations where information technology infrastructures are also well established, how much more important is children's educational success in South Korea?

2.5.1 Priority of Education in South Korea

Michael Seth (2002) once summarized education-related phenomena in South Korea as "education fever." In this society, various forms of "schooling" are not only a means to advance to upper-level schools and earn college or graduate degrees but they are also a prerequisite to enter the most prestigious schools as well as popular academic programs offered by law or medical schools. In a survey of 1,000 adults conducted by a news media and research company (Byun, 2014), 76.2% of the respondents mentioned that educational attainments would determine many important aspects of their life such as obtaining an enviable job, attracting a competent and desirable mate, establishing a sound financial foundation for a future family, supporting children, and planning for a prosperous late adulthood. By educational attainments, 58.9% of the participants meant "what school [college or university] a person attends." Most of them (71.1%) stated that entering a school of higher reputation is better than staying at one's current school, even if that meant considering a transfer or adding an extra year to start over with preparing oneself for the South Korean college entrance exam. Most South Koreans equate academic success with entering a top college.

Achieving admission to a dream college or university is primarily determined by one's score on the South Korean Scholarly Ability Test or college entrance exam, also known as the South Korean version of the SAT. To succeed in this exam is absolutely crucial for twelfth-grade students, but what makes the test even more significant is the fact that it is administered only once a year.

The exam day for 2017 was scheduled on November 16. One day before the test, however, an earthquake with a measured magnitude of 5.4 struck the southeastern regions of the Korean Peninsula. Besides its impact on students and their families, the earthquake appeared to weaken and destabilize the fourteen high school buildings in which the exam was going to be administered. The South Korean president, Moon Jae-in, finally decided to postpone the national exam for one week, which turned out to have an impact on the whole society (Kim, 2017). Similarly, Seth (2002) describes what happens typically on South Korea's national college entrance exam day. The morning commute for employees at big companies and for many government workers may be delayed for a few hours to ensure that all test-taking students arrive on time at their exam site. Police officers frequently help students who seem unable to report on time for their exam by giving them rides in police vehicles. Moreover, around the time when students are taking listening comprehension questions for their English language test, all airports across the country stop planes from taking off so that they will not make any disturbing noises. These examples vividly show how important the national college entrance exam is on both the individual and societal levels.

2.5.2 Early and Middle Childhood

In order to achieve academic excellence, many South Korean students try to learn such major subjects as math and English before they are actually attending school. For instance, preschool-aged children try to acquire, as a minimum, all math skills taught at the first-grade level and possibly up to third grade prior to actually becoming first graders. For some competitive sixth graders, their goal for math is to study and master Algebra 2, although that is a subject usually for tenth or eleventh graders. Likewise, some tenth graders are already preparing themselves for the college entrance exam in mathematics (Kim, 2018).

As for English, children's learning experiences not rarely start in an "English kindergarten," particularly in Seoul's Gangnam district. South Korea is neither an English-speaking country nor even situated near one. However, English skills are so important for South Koreans as one piece of evidence of academic excellence that people with good English skills are quite proud of themselves. Many parents want to help their children learn English as early as possible to become fluent in it as much as they can. They enroll their three-year-old children in an "English kindergarten," private English teaching institutions known as cram schools for younger children. All teachers are native English speakers and students are only allowed to use English while they are involved in their daily learning activities. Although English education at public schools only begins in third grade, "serious" parents send their children to a private English cram school far earlier. Moreover, they do so in spite of extremely expensive monthly tuitions that, on average, are equivalent to about 1,000 USD (Lee, 2012; Lee, 2018).

To help children master two or three years of advanced math curriculum or to provide them with English kindergarten experiences as early as possible are goals for many parents, although only a limited number of children succeed in achieving them. As for math, not all young students can achieve higher grade levels of skills. And in regard to English, only a small percentage of families can financially support their children in early English learning. In such cases, many students try to learn advanced math skills taught one grade above their own. Others attend ordinary cram schools for English where not all teachers are native speakers nor are the children required to use English exclusively. Nevertheless, a survey conducted in 2014 by the Korean Educational Development Institute (KEDI) showed that about 84% to 90% of all parents with children ranging from elementary to high school students ($n = 9,720$) wished for their children to complete advanced learning in math and English (Korean Educational Development Institute, 2017). Among elementary school students' parents, almost half (47.8%) stated that their children had been involved in advanced learning in English and 37.7% of them in math. In another survey in 2011, 76% of all elementary school students ($n = 1,009$) answered that they are participating in an advanced learning program in math (No Worry, 2014).

Note that this advanced learning is not available in regular schools. Because many parents and students want to study math and English at an advanced pace but schools only offer regular curricula based on the official sequence of grades, attending cram schools after the regular school day is over is a quite common activity. According to a survey conducted in 2015 (Korea Consumer Agency, 2015), among 3,000 parents of school-aged children, some 66% of them mentioned that their children started attending cram schools, often beginning in first grade. Among the attendees, more than 70% of students attended their cram school(s) three or more days a week. The top two programs that those elementary school students were participating in were English (73.5%) and math (54.8%), followed by music (37.6%) and athletics (32.9%). The other four programs were Korean language art (22.2%), fine art (like painting) (22%), writing (13.8%), and sciences (11.3%). This indicates that many South Korean elementary school students are enrolled in two or more after-school programs offered by cram schools. Therefore, every day numerous shuttle buses wait for students who take them to various cram schools just after they have been dismissed from their regular school. As a result, more than half (52.7%) of the elementary students have only two or three hours of leisure time a day. Another survey by the National Youth Commission (2005) showed that the top two things that elementary students want to do after they return home from school are to take a rest at home (61.2%) and to play with friends (48.7%), but what they actually do is go to cram schools (54.3%) and do their homework (53.4%).

Almost all South Korean elementary school students use information technology devices. In a survey done by Good Neighbor's South Korean Branch (Yu, 2017) with 1,579 elementary school students from fourth to sixth grade, most students (86.5%) had a smartphone of their own. On average, these students used their phone for four hours on weekdays, and during close to one-half of those hours (47.9%), they were listening to music or watching video clips. They spent another 30% of those hours playing smartphone games and 12.7% using social networking services.

To sum up: South Korean parents know the importance of academic success and consequently enroll their elementary school children in multiple programs in cram schools, often starting in their first-grade year. After finishing their regular classes, many of those students go directly to their cram schools and do extra work to excel and surpass the pace of their school-based curriculum. While completing their homework, students often use their smartphones to listen to music, watch video clips, play smartphone games, and use various social networking services.

2.5.3 Adolescence

Continuing their earlier lifestyle, South Korean adolescents make many extra efforts to earn good grades and develop themselves academically in order to enter highly competitive high schools (if they are in middle school) or prestigious colleges/universities (if they are high school students).

For some middle school students who are at the top of their classes, entering one of a few specialized high schools (South Koreans call these schools "High School of Science" and "Foreign Language High School") in their city or province is their most important priority. For example, eighth-grade students who are preparing themselves for the top high school entrance exam(s) spend about seven to eight hours per day in cram schools following their regular school hours. Consequently, many cram school classes end after midnight on numerous days. The students know that those attending the leading ten high schools have the best chance to be admitted to Seoul National University, South Korea's most highly regarded university. Many people believe that these top middle school students were relentlessly pushed from early childhood on, as described in the previous section. In order that their children may advance in math by mastering tenth-grade topics and skills while attending sixth grade, for instance, some parents are paying extremely high tuitions for cram school programs, and their children study excessively hard (Kim, 2018).

If this description depicts only some examples of top students' lives, what are other students' lives like? Two phenomena that can explain adolescents' daily routine are *hagwons* (cram schools) and "Late Night Self-Study Schools," which some international media have highlighted for Western audiences (Ripley, 2011; *The Economist*, 2015). Typical high school students go to school around 7:30 to 8:00 AM, where they attend regular classes until 4:00 PM. Following this, many schools provide two supplementary classes focusing on core subjects such as Korean Language Art, English, math, or sciences. Around 6:00 PM, after all of these classes are over, many tenth-grade students (who are actually first-year students at a high school) can go back home or attend their cram schools. However, high school juniors and seniors should return to school by 7:00 PM to start their "Late Night Self-Study" that usually lasts until 10:00–11:00 PM. Many *hagwons* offer classes after that. Other students who prefer more individualized lessons meet their tutors to get more help for their academic performances. South Korean high school students generally go to bed one or two hour(s) after midnight (Chun, 2004).

2.5.4 Mom: My Child Cannot Be Left Behind

Pursuing academic excellence can explain many behaviors, practices, and lifestyles of South Korean parents and children. However, trying to achieve a very high score on the national college entrance exam in order to attend a top college or university does not present a full account of the forces behind the South Korean education fever. People frequently say that the elite schools in higher education are just the top three universities (Seoul National University, Yonsei University, and Korea University) or, at most, the top five. Whereas the total annual number of students that these schools can admit as their freshmen class is between 15,000 and 20,000, the annual number of test takers for the entrance exam is at present around 600,000 (Yoo, 2017). Should we, therefore, conclude that most parents and students in South Korea only compete against each other so that they may score among the top 2.5%~3% on the national college entrance exam?

One of the most common goals of the parents, particularly those whose children score in the top 10% nationally, is to strongly support their children so they will not fall behind their peers. For instance, when children are in kindergarten or first grade, if some parents begin sending their children to *hagwons*, the other parents will follow suit. Even though South Korean kindergartens or elementary schools do not reveal students' class rankings to anybody these days, parental concern for children's academic success starts right then (Korea Consumer Agency, 2015).

2.5.5 Related Phenomena Stemming from Extreme Competitiveness in Education

Because educational success is a central goal for almost all, every aspect of national educational policies, particularly with respect to the national college entrance exam and how to assess the overall achievements/abilities of students, regularly attracts people's scrutiny. This is one reason that South Korea's Department of Education takes charge of the college entrance exam and policy for all levels of education. That is to say, students and parents want the government to create and maintain a competitive system that is as fair and objective as possible (Nam, 2017). For instance, they would dislike it if teachers' recommendation letters, students' personal essays or statements, or any volunteering records would be considered seriously as part of the college admission screening process. After all, such considerations lead to an increased possibility of involving potentially unfair considerations because subjective standards may be employed when candidates are evaluated by admission officers. People generally consider getting a better test score on the college entrance exam as a more objective and fairer criterion than any other. They also believe that the government should implement and control the college entrance exam rather than allowing each college and university to develop its own ways to evaluate applicants' achievements and abilities.

Since South Koreans share a common interest in education, any effective strategy outlining how their children could earn a better score on exams and how they could attain admission to their dream school quickly gains great popularity. A big business industry exists in which "experts in education" or "professionals for the entrance exam" establish certain strategies and apply them in their cram schools or tutoring lessons. In the capital, Seoul, there are a couple of districts such as Gangnam where one can find several hundred "expert" *hagwons* competing against each other. Mothers of school-aged children and teenagers respect and envy those who are knowledgeable about different strategies and know how to create effective programs. There is a saying among South Koreans that "a child's academic success is an outcome of his or her mom's information and knowledge about study skills and college admission strategy."

Moreover, unusual success stories where a student's family cannot afford private cram schools or tutoring opportunities, yet their child is tremendously successful on the college entrance exam – such as achieving a perfect score – soon become very popular. A few of these students have attracted the attention of the media and even become celebrities (Oh, 2018).

In order to be admitted to the college or university of their dreams, children and adolescents challenge themselves every day, and their parents do not hesitate to invest vast amounts of money into their children's cram schools and private tutoring lessons. This whole situation obviously creates highly stressful circumstances for students. For instance, the 2011 suicide rate for South Korean youth (ages ten to twenty-four years) was 9.4 per 100,000 persons. This made it the sixth highest rate among the current thirty-five Organisation for Economic Co-operation and Development (OECD) member countries. According to a 2012 report from Statistics Korea (Statistics Korea, 2012), committing suicide was the most frequent reason for adolescents' deaths (27.3%), followed by traffic accidents (20%). In a survey in 2014 with 7,465 children and adolescents (National Youth Policy Institute, 2014), about 30% of the respondents mentioned that they had thought about suicide in the past year. The most important reasons for this suicidal ideation were their school grades and their class rankings (42.7%). Another survey in 2014 by the Korea Health Promotion Institute (2014) found that 29.1% of South Korean teenagers (aged from fourteen to nineteen years) had felt severely depressed during the previous thirty days, and the number one reason was again their academic performance and ranking in their classes (40%). For so many of these students, the national entrance examination represents what many Koreans (and Japanese) prefer to call Examination Hell.

2.5.6 The Uncertain Future of South Korean Education Fever

Despite the idiosyncratic nature of South Koreans' passion and struggle for educational success, the country's reduced birth rate is about to lead to some dramatic consequences for its education system and its competitiveness. The total number of twelfth graders who took the college entrance exam was close to 900,000 during the years 1998 through 2001, but then it began a sharp decline to between 600,000 and 650,000 after 2014. Moreover, those numbers are expected to shrink even further and hit the 500,000s by 2020 and the 400,000s by 2021 or 2022. This dramatic decrease in the student population is likely to make it next to impossible for about 60 (or 30%) out of 197 colleges and universities in South Korea to find any applicants in the very near future (Kim, 2018). South Korean education and with it the whole society are about to face an enormous challenge!

3 Comparing Families, Children, and Adolescents in Four Types of Evolving Societies

This section provides concise summaries of the basic nature of families, children, and adolescents in the four types of evolving societies under discussion. The summaries are based on the four specific societies just described as well as on various comparable societies falling within the scope of each of the four societal categories.

3.1 Families

Table 3.1 summarizes the nature of families in small-scale foraging bands, nomadic pastoralist societies, peasant societies, and digital information societies. In foraging bands, patrilineal kinship systems (descent and inheritance go through the male bloodline) and bilateral kinship systems (descent and inheritance follow both male and female lines) occur most commonly. Although most men have only one wife, polygyny (a husband has two or more wives) can be found among some Australian Aboriginal groups. Polygyny tends to reinforce distinctively defined gender roles as well as gender- and age-related

Table 3.1 Families in Four Types of Society

	Small-scale foraging bands	Nomadic pastoralist societies	Peasant societies	Digital information societies
Marriage Systems and Postmarital Residence	Patrilineal and bilateral kinship most common; monogamy and some polygyny; patrilocal or multi-local residence	Patrilineal descent and patrilocal residence common; polygyny for the well-off and powerful	Patrilineal descent most common but matrilineal descent especially in some horticultural societies; polygyny (for the well-off) and patrilocal residence both common	Monogamy and neolocal residence widespread; polygyny illegal or else uncommon
Impact of Polygyny on Family Functioning	Polygyny increases inequality and delays marriage for young males; it reinforces age and gender role differences	Cool relationship between parents and tensions between co-wives are common; reinforces gender role differences; reduces father–child contact	Cool relationship between parents and tensions between co-wives are common; reinforces gender role differences; reduces father–child contact; exclusive mother–child households less warm; common yet declining in parts of Africa	Informally practiced in some immigrant and religious groups; endangers economic welfare of families

Mothers' vs. Fathers' Impact on Children	Mother-child contact strongest in early years; father-child contact often considerable in small bands	Father may be a remote authority figure; his impact is strongest on boys in the later stages of childhood	Father may be a remote authority figure; his impact is strongest in the later stages of childhood	Father's presence increasing in two-parent, middle-class families but declining in single-mother families (which are on the increase)
Family Size and Fertility Rates (TFR)	Moderate family sizes; fairly high to high fertility rates	Rather large families; rather high fertility rates; pronatalist ideologies	Large families; high fertility rates; pronatalist ideologies	Small nuclear families; TFRs = 1.2–1.9 and thus below replacement rate (2.1)
Family Stability and Structures	Moderate family stability; early divorces common; extensive husband–wife interaction	Family stability often fairly high; polygyny, extended families, and patrilineal clans common	Often low divorce rates; fewer single-parent families; extended families especially among the well-to-do; family instability in some sub-Saharan countries	Medium to high divorce rates; many single-parent and childless families; increased variety of family types; many young adult singles
Economic Activities and Functions of Family	Families perform all main economic activities	Wide range of economic activities, including herding and trade	Wide range of economic activities, especially in subsistence economies and among peasants	Families are shedding many economic functions

Table 3.1 (cont.)

	Small-scale foraging bands	Nomadic pastoralist societies	Peasant societies	Digital information societies
Socialization/Teaching Functions of Family; Alloparenting and Polymatric Care	Alloparenting by grandmothers, other adults, and older girls who help rear, protect, and teach children	Extensive socialization and teaching by nuclear and extended family members such as grandmothers	Pervasive influence of family members, including grandparents, but teaching functions now shifting toward schools	Many family functions are being transferred to schools, preschools, and daycare centers; grandparents influence tends to be positive
Parental Reasons for Having Children	It is traditional; economic utility, provides support in old age; emotional companionship; a spiritual goal; children validate adult identity	It is traditional; economic utility, provides support in old age; add to families' political influence; provides emotional companionship; a spiritual goal; children manifest God's blessing; children validate adult status and social identity	It is traditional; economic utility; provides support in old age; add to families' political influence; emotional companionship; a spiritual goal; children manifest God's blessing; children validate adult status and social identity	Children provide emotional companionship but are expensive to raise; having children is an individual preference competing with other preferences that are influenced by consumerism, long years of schooling, and focus on careers

inequalities. After marriage, many couples join the husband's group (patrilocal residence) and take on the husband's name, although the composition of foraging bands tends to be fluid and multi-local residence occurs rather frequently. Family sizes in such societies are often moderate in spite of high fertility rates. Divorces commonly occur, and in such cases the younger children tend to stay with the mother. The practice of alloparenting or joint parenting, especially by grandmothers, the mother's sisters, and older female siblings, is common and tends to have positive effects on children. Parents in foraging bands like to have children because they hope that their children will provide some economic support for the family and take care of them as they grow older and more fragile, and because their children provide companionship.

Both nomadic pastoralist societies and peasant societies tend to favor patrilineal descent and patrilocal residence (the wife lives with or near her husband's family) while polygyny is often practiced by the more powerful men. This can easily lead to problems between competing co-wives while the amount of father–child contact tends to be on the low side. The father is more likely to be a factor in the lives of his older sons, but during their early years, he may see little of them or his daughters. Exclusive mother–child households also tend to be characterized by less emotional warmth (Rohner, 1975). Matrilineal descent (descent and inheritance follow the female bloodline) and matrilocal residence (the husband lives with or near his wife's family) do sometimes occur in relatively small horticultural/agricultural and a few pastoralist societies. While such societies tend to be more equal in terms of gender-linked status and roles, males nevertheless tend to assume political leadership roles in them. Sometimes, a wife's older brother has more authority vis-à-vis his sister's children than their actual father who, however, tends to be emotionally involved in their lives. Pastoralists and even more so peasants tend to have high fertility rates and large families. Most parents want several children because they expect them to contribute to their family's economic and political welfare, they will keep the family name alive, and they manifest God's blessings. A woman's most important duty is to conceive and raise many children. Most of these families are pretty stable, often function within the context of extended families, and tend to be characterized by supportive relationships between grandmothers and children. Children learn by observing and interacting with members of their immediate and extended families. However, schools have been gaining in importance in many of these societies and are taking over the formal teaching of children.

In the digital information societies, monogamous relationships predominate. After being married, most couples choose a neolocal residence and live separately from their families of origin. Neolocal residence tends to weaken the influence of other family members, especially in those cases where they live far away. However, when grandparents live nearby, they often enjoy warm relationships with their grandchildren. Except for various Islamic societies, polygyny is mostly considered illegal, although a few immigrants may surreptitiously practice it. However, in advanced Islamic societies, polygyny is becoming less prevalent as well. Except for a few religious groups, family sizes have shrunk continuously based on very low fertility rates. Many children now attend a sequence of preschools, schools, and colleges or universities, whereas in former times they would have been taught at home or attended school for just a few years. Thus, the financial contributions of today's children to the family budget tend to be low, while the family must finance much of their education over the course of many years.

3.2 Children

Table 3.2 compares children in four types of societies. Three of these, small-scale foraging bands, nomadic pastoralists, and peasant societies, share several childhood characteristics. Thus, child mortality rates were until recently very high, and life expectancies low, due to infections, diseases, the nonexistence or unavailability of essential vaccinations, accidents, periodic famines, and sometimes warfare. During the infancy and toddlerhood years, breastfeeding and co-sleeping are part of the children's lives until the children are about two to four years old. Such societies do not have preschool or daycare centers; instead, their children learn by observing their surroundings, through play, by actively participating in family activities, and by practicing under the guidance of older siblings and adults. Older sisters often spend more time with their younger siblings than their mothers, who may be busy working in the fields, milking animals, fetching water, and doing housework.

However, in small-scale foraging bands, young children are encouraged to practice self-reliance and independence from an early age, and they are not expected to be that obedient (Barry, Child, & Bacon, 1959; Lew-Levy et al., 2018). Their activities in playgroups are mostly self-directed. Moreover, self-reliance and independence training, especially for boys, can also be found among many pastoralist societies. In contrast, obedience training tends to prevail in peasant societies, and especially so for girls.

The children of many nomadic pastoralist and peasant societies already assume a variety of responsibilities at an early age by taking care of small animals, helping out at home, and performing simple agricultural tasks. Girls in particular are often expected to take care of and supervise younger siblings.

Table 3.2 Children in Four Types of Society

	Small-scale foraging bands	Nomadic pastoralist societies	Peasant societies	Digital information societies
Child Mortality Rates and Life Expectancies	Very high child mortality rates and low life expectancies due to diseases, hunting accidents, attacks by animals, and sometimes conflicts and warfare	High (but declining) child mortality rates and low life expectancies due to diseases, accidents, famines, and periodic warfare	High (but declining) child mortality rates and low life expectancies due to diseases, famines, and wars within and between societies	Lowest child mortality rates and highest life expectancies in history due to modern medicine and life conditions
Infancy: Breastfeeding and Co-Sleeping	Frequent on-demand breastfeeding for several years; extensive skin-to-skin contact and co-sleeping	Breastfeeding often for two–three years; co-sleeping is widespread	Breastfeeding often for two–four years; co-sleeping is common	Breastfeeding often for less than one year; variable skin-to-skin contact; variable and time-limited co-sleeping
Early Childhood	Considerable freedom to explore non-dangerous environments; considerable autonomy and self-reliant behavior; little physical punishment; multiple caregivers	Increasingly structured, especially for girls; physical punishment is rather common; early assumption of selected responsibilities	Increasingly structured, especially for girls; physical punishment is rather common, especially for boys; emphasis on children's obedience and early learning of responsibilities	Children's environments are often regulated yet increasing emphasis on self-esteem and self-determination; decreasing outdoor exploration and activities in cities

Table 3.2 (cont.)

	Small-scale foraging bands	Nomadic pastoralist societies	Peasant societies	Digital information societies
Attendance of Preschools, Daycare Centers	None: children learn by observation, play, practice, and from everybody	None: children learn by observation and practice and from siblings	Uncommon: children learn by observation, play, practice and from siblings	Expanding attendance; emphasis on early preparation for schools
Self-Reliance and Independence Training	Often pronounced for boys, fairly high for girls	Pronounced for boys, moderate for girls	Low, especially for girls	High, especially in individualistic societies that encourage children's assertiveness and questioning behavior
Obedience and Responsibility Training	Limited emphasis, but higher for girls; sharing is often emphasized	Moderate to high, especially for girls, who tend to be more obedient, responsible, and nurturing	Prevalent above all for girls, who tend to be more obedient, responsible, and nurturing	Variable and decreasing
Recognition of Five–Seven Shift	Yes: children increasingly expected to understand the world	Yes: children increasingly expected to understand the world and their duties	Yes: children increasingly expected to understand the world and their duties	Yes: children sent to elementary school

Child Work in Middle Childhood	Young children acquire adult skills in semi-playful and noncompetitive ways; limited emphasis on rigid work activities	Child work is common: children perform many adult responsibilities starting early in life	Most children work at home and in the fields; exploitative child labor is rather common	Little preteen child work (part-time jobs for some teenagers)
Age Segregation of Children and Adolescents	Very limited segregation; mixed-age groups common	Moderate, although adolescent age sets are common in parts of Africa	Moderate; adolescent age sets common in parts of Africa	Considerable (both voluntary and due to schooling)
Number and Influence of Siblings	Moderate number of siblings who exert moderate influence on younger children	Moderate number of siblings and stepsiblings who may have considerable influence	Many siblings; girls often involved in childrearing duties; early responsibility training by older siblings is common	Few siblings; often limited sibling influence (but more in poor families); individualistic childrearing approaches
Schooling and Literacy	Traditionally none; teaching and learning embedded in everyday contexts	Traditionally uncommon, especially for girls; instead learning in everyday environments and on the job	Illiteracy and semiliteracy were widespread among peasant children (especially girls) but are now declining; girls' education contested in some Islamic societies	Universal schooling for both boys and girls; Pre-K education expanding; most teenagers enrolled in school; tertiary education expanding; learning about remote events, activities, and places is common

Table 3.2 (cont.)

	Small-scale foraging bands	Nomadic pastoralist societies	Peasant societies	Digital information societies
Social Relations with Kin and Strangers	Long-term relations with kin and ingroup members; limited or no exposure to strangers	Long-term relations with kin and ingroup members; exposure to strangers is increasing	Long-term relations with kin and ingroup members; exposure to strangers is increasing	Emphasis on nuclear family; numerous interactions with non-kin strangers and semi-strangers
Privacy for Children and Adolescents	Little privacy, life takes place in the open	Little privacy for tent dwellers, life takes place in the open	Often little or limited privacy	Increasing privacy, especially for adolescents in individualistic societies
Children's Exposure to Warfare, Civil War, and Guerrillas	War and violence less common between small bands but common among larger nomadic societies	Warfare was common between many nomadic tribes and with agriculturalists but is now mostly controlled by states	Fairly common in the Middle East and Africa; children may be abducted and forced to become soldiers and "war brides"	Rare in recent decades
Recent Impact of HIV/AIDS on Families and Children	Occasional impact due to interaction with outsiders	Occasional impact due to interaction with outsiders, especially in southern Africa	Powerful threat, especially in southern Africa, responsible for numerous orphans; less prevalent in Muslim societies; both female and male victims	Limited except among drug users, homosexuals, and prostitutes; victims mostly male

When compared to boys, they usually are assigned more chores. This was found by Whiting and Edwards (1988), for instance, who focused on four-to-ten-year-old children across six cultures. Child work typically intensifies in middle childhood (supported by the cognitive and probably universal "five-to-seven transition"), when new responsibilities are assigned (Rogoff et al., 1975) and children are expected to acquire new skills and knowledge in everyday situations. At the same time, they are surrounded by many family members and are expected to develop strong relationships with them as well as with other members of their local group. Thus, they learn to adapt to face-to-face communities while performing many subsistence activities.

In digital information societies, however, child mortality rates are very low, thereby reflecting advancements in medicine and health care practices. Furthermore, many children are breastfed for shorter periods of time and co-sleeping has become less common in individualistic societies such as the United States, although it remains a frequent and advisable practice in more collectivistic societies such as Japan and South Korea. Given their mainly urban surroundings and TV watching habits, many children now spend only a limited amount of time in the outdoors. Often, they have few if any siblings and consequently, girls in particular are much less involved in sibling care and other nurturing activities when compared to typical preindustrial societies. Instead, a growing emphasis exists on young children attending preschool and daycare centers for educational reasons, or else because the mother is working.

Regarding the basic nature of children's lives, throughout most of prehistory and history, middle and late childhood constituted the periods when children were perfecting the skills they would soon need to make clothes, go hunting, run households, supervise their future children, perform basic agricultural tasks, herd smaller and larger animals, and defend themselves against wild animals and perhaps brigands and hostile neighbors. Such lives contrast in striking ways with those led by children and many young adults in digital information societies, who until their twenties (and sometimes even their thirties), spend a crucial part of their time in educational institutions in order to acquire the types of knowledge most valued in their technological societies. However, unlike quite a few of their peers, especially in the more isolated and rural areas of poorer countries, they usually are not able to distinguish between hundreds of wild plants, including those possessing medicinal value, ride horses at full speed, milk cows and *dri* (female yaks), cultivate manioc, weave their own clothes, help prepare meals, or hunt wild animals with the help of spears, bows and poisoned arrows, or blow guns. Thus, they lack the practical skills, practical knowledge, and certain interpersonal skills

(Greenfield et al., 2003) that the largely illiterate children of former generations would routinely acquire through observation, imitation, practice, and guidance by their older siblings and elders. Consequently, a trade-off exists between acquiring survival and social skills honed through years of actual practice as opposed to knowledge learned from teachers, books, and the Internet. In traditional societies, children, adolescents, and adults typically acquire competence in the first realm but lack exposure in the second realm. In contrast, modern children and adults are likely to fit the opposite pattern: they have limited survival skills but go through numerous years of learning school-related skills. These patterns constitute different forms of adjustment to different kinds of ecological and technological settings. However, when children coached in survival skills such as traditional Aboriginal children are sent to modern schools in order to acquire a variety of symbolic cognitive skills needed in the modern world, they may experience psychosocial and intellectual difficulties, fall behind, and perhaps drop out. More generally, students in educational institutions learn to think in more abstract ways, gain access to written materials, become numerate, are exposed to scientific ways of thinking, become aware of situations and whole worlds outside their immediate environment, and are supported in their ability to perceive and distinguish between various expanding options in their lives. Thus, formal schooling tends to leave a powerful impact on children's minds.

3.3 Adolescents

Table 3.3 compares adolescents in four types of society. Among small-scale foraging bands, the length of the adolescent period tends to be brief and girls often have their menarche fairly late. About 60% of all hunter-gatherer groups practice some form of initiation ceremonies, which are often performed for both males and females (Schlegel & Barry, 1991). Such rituals are found in many Australian groups but less so in small African bands, where many boys get married at an earlier age. While both arranged and semi-arranged marriages can be found in foraging societies, the emphasis on premarital chastity for girls or boys tends to be low. Diseases and accidents are an important threat and can lead to fairly high mortality rates among adolescents. Traditionally, the members of such societies were illiterate and mass media were unknown to them, although that is changing now.

Compared to their peers in peasant societies, pastoralist male teenagers enjoy more independence and freedom while they are performing their demanding and sometimes dangerous tasks. In both types of societies, such as in many age-graded agricultural and pastoralist societies in Africa, public,

Table 3.3 Adolescents in Four Types of Society

	Small-scale foraging bands	Nomadic pastoralist societies	Peasant societies	Digital information societies
Length of Adolescent Period, Time of Menarche	Brief adolescent period, especially for girls; late menarche if limited food supply	Fairly brief period, especially for girls; menarche may be fairly late among high-altitude nomads	Variable: Brief or barely existing for many girls; late menarche because of low-protein diet; brief period for boys, but prolonged in African polygamous and age-graded societies	Extended adolescence often followed by "emerging adulthood" period (eighteen–twenty-six years); early menarche because of improved diet
Puberty and Adulthood Rites	Less common in the smaller groups but frequent in larger Australian groups	Common, demanding, often painful, especially for boys, may be dramatic, male and female circumcision common in the Middle East and Africa; more private circumcision rituals for girls	Common, demanding, often painful, especially for boys, may be dramatic, male and female circumcision common in the Middle East and Africa; more private circumcision rituals for girls	Selective, voluntary, less common, and less painful rites (e.g., *quinceañera*)

Table 3.3 (cont.)

	Small-scale foraging bands	Nomadic pastoralist societies	Peasant societies	Digital information societies
Age of Marriage for Girls	Low to fairly low	Often rather low	May be very low (ten–twenty years), but often was very late in preindustrial Europe; now later due to spread of schooling	Increasing (mean = twenty-four to thirty years); more ambivalence about marriage; motherhood less emphasized
Are Marriages Arranged or Semi-Arranged?	Variable	Mostly yes	Mostly yes	Mostly no, sometimes go-betweens (Japan)
Value of Premarital Chastity for Girls	Low; sexual play in childhood rather common	Premarital chastity emphasized, especially in Islamic societies, variable in traditional African societies, girls kept closer to home	Very high in Middle Eastern, Muslim, and Hindu (*purdah*) societies; high in Confucian-heritage societies, variable in sub-Saharan societies; girls kept closer to home	Rapidly declining in most Western societies (e.g., Scandinavia) and increasingly so in some East Asian societies
Age of Marriage for Boys	Rather low but variable	Variable but often fairly low; late marriage in some age-graded societies	Variable but increasing; higher in many polygamous societies	Late marriages; more ambivalence about institution of marriage

				and in preindustrial Europe
Knowledge and Value Differences between Generations	Formerly few differences	Limited differences but now increasing due to schooling and global influences	Limited but increasing differences due to schooling, modernization, and global influences	Pervasive differences especially in the knowledge areas, less so for basic values
Peer Group Influence	Low to moderate	Moderate to fairly high	Moderate (although strong for males in some age-graded African societies)	Pervasive for both males and females
Adolescents' Exposure to Mass Media	Traditionally none	Traditionally none (but now increasing)	Limited (especially for girls) but becoming widespread	Pervasive
Adolescent Subcultures	Rare	Subcultures exist in some nomadic societies	Especially in age-graded societies; otherwise emerging in schools and bigger cities	Widespread and increasingly influenced by social and mass media
Impact of Global Teenage Culture(s)	Originally very limited but growing	Limited but growing	Growing via media influence and leading to more "glocal" identities	Powerful: many adolescents are becoming semi-multicultural
Impact of Consumerism on Children's and Adolescents' Lifestyles	Originally none but now emerging	Limited but growing	Struggle for survival limits consumerism for the poor	Strong impact on lifestyles and identities

Table 3.3 (cont.)

	Small-scale foraging bands	Nomadic pastoralist societies	Peasant societies	Digital information societies
Adolescent Self: More Individualistic or More Collectivistic?	Moderately individualistic self	More individualistic self than in peasant societies, especially among boys	Collectivistic self is embedded in kin and other face-to-face social networks; more individualism in cities	Individualistic self is linked to personal preferences and lifestyles, especially in Western societies; individualism increasing worldwide
Societal Threats to Children's and Adolescents' Welfare	Some infanticide; poor understanding of childhood diseases, internal fighting inside and between larger groups	Infanticide; slavery; killings, rape, abductions, and abandonment, especially during war times; boy soldiers	Infanticide; serfdom and slavery; excessive child labor; very early marriage, especially for girls; sexual abuse and forced prostitution for poor girls; dangerous slum environments; high homicide rates, especially in Central America	Sexual abuse of girls and some boys; parental negligence; extreme poverty and dangerous slum environments (e. g., in the United States); increasing obesity lowers life expectancies

painful, and dramatic circumcision rituals are frequently performed for groups of boys (Beckwith & Fisher, 1999). The rituals provide instruction in adult sex roles, support cultural loyalty, increase cohesion among peers and between adolescents and same-sex adults, and announce a new social status for its participants. Girls' circumcision or genital mutilation is more likely to be a private family affair. Some of its forms such as infibulation or "Pharaonic circumcision" are extremely painful yet continue to be carried out, especially in the rural areas of some North African countries such as Sudan. Intended to protect girls' premarital chastity, infibulation involves the removal or the sealing of the labia majora and the labia minora together after the entire clitoris has been removed (Ahmed & Gielen, 2017: 97). More generally, unmarried female teenagers are frequently required to refrain from sexual intercourse in order to protect their reputation, their chances of getting married, and their price in marriage transactions. Young maids and other servants, however, can be vulnerable to sexual exploitation, and very poor girls in particular may be induced or forced to engage in prostitution.

In general, the female experience of adolescence in pastoralist and peasant societies begins about two years earlier when compared to that of their male counterparts. Nevertheless and because of their limited diets, female teenagers often have their menarche relatively late, namely around an average age of thirteen to seventeen years. Their adolescence tends be more toned down than that of their male peers because females are kept closer to home, are more involved in helping out in the household, and are more subordinate to their fathers, mothers, and grandparents. They are also less likely to develop a distinct youth culture and to enjoy some form of autonomy (Mawhinney, 2015). Moreover, marriages are frequently arranged and tend to reflect the economic, political, sociocultural, and status concerns of clans and extended families rather than the preferences and feelings of the future spouses. Many girls get married at fairly low ages, although this was not the case in many of Europe's preindustrial and usually poor societies. In most peasant and pastoralist societies, both younger and older adolescents are routinely engaged in labor. Girls are more likely to be involved in unpaid household labor whereas boys from poor families are asked to perform income-generating labor in the outside world (e.g., Cain, 1980, for rural Bangladesh).

Whereas in former years major cultural and psychosocial differences between the generations had been uncommon, the modern expansion of schooling and the intensifying impact of global influences are now leading to increased knowledge and value differences between the generations in both

types of societies. Consequently, new adolescent ways of behaving and thinking are emerging in these societies, such as among peer groups in the schools.

One important difference between the traditional nomadic and peasant
societies is that in the pastoralist societies, adolescents are/were more likely
to be killed, abducted, and/or raped, especially in the context of rather frequent
wars and local conflicts. Crime rates and serious personal conflicts in such
societies can vary considerably, yet their frequency may be high. When wars or
local uprisings occur among and between agrarian and nomadic societies, they
do at times result in deadly famines that cause the death of a disproportionate
number of children and elderly. Moreover, wars may involve child soldiers and
young "war brides," as can be seen in some of today's African and Middle
Eastern conflicts.

In modern digital information societies, the length of the adolescent period
has been steadily expanding due to the spread of secondary and tertiary forms
of schooling. Increasingly, adolescence is followed by an exploratory period
of emerging adulthood (from about eighteen to twenty-six years), during
which young people remain unmarried and often continue with their education. Especially in East Asian societies, most adolescents spend large
amounts of time on educational tasks but much less on chores. They have
less free time than their North American peers (cf. Larson & Verma, 1999,
p. 725). Going to school leads to exposure to previously unknown adults and
peers outside one's family. Since diets have been much improved, girls
frequently have their menarche in the beginning teenage years. Adolescent
rites of passage tend to be less physically taxing, less common, and more
voluntary in nature than those practiced in many preindustrial societies.
Males and females get married at much later ages, arranged marriages are
becoming uncommon, and the value of girls' premarital chastity has been
declining substantially in many Western and some East Asian societies,
although not in the Islamic world. Considerable generational differences
have been emerging in areas such as information processing skills, together
with the emergence of adolescent subcultures that reflect the influence of
peers as well as the pervasive impact of rapidly changing mass media. Many
modern adolescents are exposed to a variety of multicultural forces that may
induce them to entertain new ideas and values, while reinforcing more
individualistic identities and preconceptions. At the same time, some adolescents in the digital information societies suffer from parental negligence, are
forced to grow up in dangerous slums, or are exposed to alcohol and dangerous drugs. Across various nations, the risk of obesity has been steadily
increasing due to adolescents' ready access to a broad variety of potentially
unhealthy kinds of food.

4 Global Changes in Childhood and Adolescence

4.1 Twelve Diverse Countries Spanning the Globe

In the following, we note a number of demographic, economic, and educational trends that are exerting a major influence on the lives of children and youth all around the world. To better understand the broad nature of these trends, we initially selected twelve nations representing the major world regions. They differ widely from each other with respect to their histories, size, economic status, political systems, cultural and educational traditions, and religious beliefs. Table 4.1 presents selected demographic indicators for these twelve countries.

In terms of numbers, the countries are led by China and India, two Asian low- to medium-income nations where 32.4% of the world's children live. The United States takes its place in the table as the most populous Western, well-to-do country, and Indonesia as the largest predominantly Muslim nation. Brazil and Mexico are listed as the two biggest Latin American countries, while Nigeria and Ethiopia represent two poor African nations with large and rapidly growing populations. Egypt is included as the most populous Arab country, Russia as the largest Eastern European/North Asian country, and Germany as the most populous, well-to-do European nation. Two additional nations, South Korea and Guatemala, appear in the table because children living in these two smaller countries were described earlier. Altogether, the 1.211 billion children residing in these twelve nations make up 52.8% of the world's children (cf. Gielen, 2016).

The twelve countries vary greatly in their per capita incomes, which have been adjusted for purchasing power parity. This means that the reported incomes take into account national differences in relative cost of living and inflation rates in order to make them more comparable. The two poorest countries in the table are Ethiopia and Nigeria, which report much higher TFRs than any of the other countries. At the same time, the data point to very high levels of underweight and stunting among their young children below the age of five, especially when compared to those living in economically better-off countries. However, India, the nation with by far the world's largest number of children, reports even higher rates of stunting than the two African countries. More generally, the world's two major regions for child poverty and the negative physical and psychosocial consequences associated with it are sub-Saharan Africa and South Asia.

By way of contrast, the three richest countries included in the table are the United States, Germany, and South Korea. While stunting is rare in those nations, their TFRs have now sunk below the "replacement rate" of 2.1 children

Table 4.1 Selected Demographic Indicators for Twelve Representative Countries

Country	Population 2018*	Children <18 years (2016)**	GDP (PPP) in US$ (2017)*	TFR * (2017)	Underweight children <5 years old (2017)*
China	1.415 billion	295 million	16,000	1.60	3.4% (2010)
India	1.354 billion	448 million	7,200	2.43	35.7% (2015)
United States	327 million	73 million	59,500	1.87	0.5% (2012)
Indonesia	267 million	86 million	12,400	2.11	19.9% (2013)
Brazil	211 million	56 million	15,500	1.75	2.2% (2007)
Nigeria	196 million	94 million	5,900	5.07	19.4% (2015)
Russia	144 million	29 million	27,900	1.67	?
Mexico	131 million	42 million	19,500	2.24	3.9% (2015)
Ethiopia	108 million	50 million	2,100	4.99	23.6% (2016)
Egypt	99 million	37 million	13,000	3.47	7% (2014)
Germany	82 million	13 million	50,200	1.45	1.1% (2006)
South Korea	51 million	9 million	34,500	1.28	0.7% (2010)
Guatemala	15 million	7 million	8,200	2.77	12.6% (2015)
World	7.618 billion	2.295 billion	17,300[1]	2.42	14% (2016)

GDP (PPP): Per capita income adjusted for purchasing power; TFR: Total Fertility Rate

Sources: 2018: www.worldometers.info/

* CIA The World Factbook; The World Bank Group

** UNICEF The State of the World's Children 2017

[1] Index Mundi

per woman and lifetime. Such low TFRs are typical for aging information societies. Russia, a country with moderately high income levels, reports a typically European fertility rate that is low yet somewhat higher than that of well-to-do Germany. The two predominantly Muslim countries in the table, Indonesia and Egypt, report similar per capita incomes but surprisingly different rates for children's underweight and TFRs: Indonesia's present TFR stands exactly at the same level as its replacement rate, but Egypt's rate is much higher and promises major population increases for the foreseeable future. The three Latin American countries report modest to moderate income levels, declining and rather low levels of underweight for their young children, and low to fairly low TFRs. China, an economically evolving country with the second largest number of children, also reports rather low rates of stunting and a low TFR thanks to its former one child policy (which did not apply to all families), and its replacement, the country's recently established two child policy. However, like several other East Asian countries, South Korea, a well-developed information society that never adopted any kind of one child policy, has a TFR even lower than that of China.

4.2 Global Trends

The data reported in Table 4.1 form an instructive background for discussing several long-term demographic, health-related, gender-related, and educational changes that can help us understand more clearly how childhood is changing all across the globe (Gielen, 2016). It should be added in this context that among today's children, less than 0.01% come from hunter-gatherer backgrounds and only 0.4% from nomadic pastoralist families. By way of contrast, more than one-third of the world's children are growing up in predominantly agricultural environments and about 70% of all globally employed children are working in such settings (Wikipedia, 2018a). However, the majority of children nowadays resides in the rapidly expanding urban areas of poor, medium-income, and well-to-do countries rather than in rural areas.

4.2.1 The World's Population Continues to Expand Rapidly

The world's population explosion represents arguably the most dramatic and powerful change in human history. Whereas on the eve of the agricultural and pastoralist revolutions some ten to twelve millennia ago, the global population consisted of a few million hunter-gatherers, basic changes in subsistence economy led over time to enormous population increases. By the year 1802, the population had reached 1 billion, with most of them involved in agricultural pursuits (Roser & Ortiz-Ospina, 2018a). By 1959, that population had tripled to

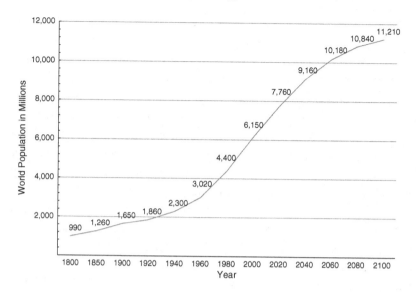

Figure 4.1 World population, 1800–2015, and projections until 2100
Source: Data derived from Max Roser & Esteban Ortiz-Ospina (2018a), *Our World in Data*: World Population Growth, 1750–2015 and Projections until 2100. https://ourworldindata.org/world-population-growth

reach 3 billion and today, in 2018, it consists of an estimated 7.6 billion persons. Moreover, the population continues to grow rapidly and may surpass 11 billion around the year 2100.

Figure 4.1 depicts global population estimates and predictions for the years 1800–2100. The numbers are taken from Roser and Ortiz-Ospina (2018a) and are likely to be reasonably close to reality, especially for recent decades. Estimates for earlier time periods are subject to larger margins of error, but the powerful upward trajectory depicted in the figure is not in doubt. Barring unforeseen circumstances, predictions about population increases for the remaining part of the twenty-first century are most trustworthy for the next few decades, but less so for the remainder of the century.

The world's continents and major regions account for quite different percentages of today's global population. They are: Asia: 62.76%; Africa: 15.96%; North and Central America: 7.8%; Europe: 7.39%; South America: 5.66%; Oceania: 0.44%. Thus, close to 79% of the world's population live in Asia and Africa, and that percentage will increase in the coming years. This is so because yearly population increases are most pronounced in the least developed countries, especially in Africa (2.32%), lower in the less developed countries (1.27%), and lowest in the more developed countries in Europe, East

Asia, and North America (0.26%). Among the latter, several countries are now shrinking in population size due to very low birth rates and, at times, out-migration. Relevant examples include Romania (−0.49% in 2015), Portugal (−0.48%), and Japan (−0.16%). The ongoing and troubling decline in the number of children and college-age students suggests a similar future for South Korea.

4.2.2 Child Mortality Rates Have Been Declining Sharply across the Globe

One of humanity's most uplifting changes during the past 160 years can be seen in the stunning decline of young children's death rates, as depicted in Figure 4.2. In 1860, for instance, an estimated 41.4% of the world's children died before they reached their fifth birthday. Whether they were the children of Australian Aborigines, Tibetan nomads, Maya peasants, or South Korean peasants, they died in large (though moderately varying) numbers due to preterm problems, birth complications, pneumonia, diarrhea, and various infectious and communicable diseases such as measles and smallpox (which alone killed an estimated 300–500 million human beings in the twentieth century before it was eradicated in the late 1970s). These diseases, in turn, were bolstered by unhygienic conditions such as unclean water and scarcity of basic toilets, a lack of modern medical knowledge and technology, absence of

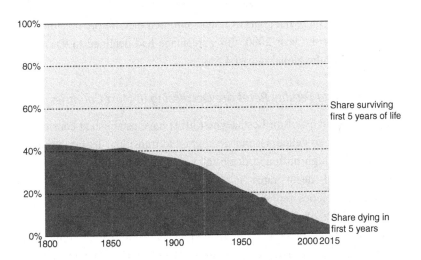

Figure 4.2 Global child mortality (share of the world's population dying and surviving the first five years of life)

Sources: Gapminder and the World Bank

vaccinations, sporadic famines, and the health-related consequences of military conflicts. In addition, a good number of infants were either killed or abandoned by their parents. Thus, in the past, the study of children too often meant the study of death.

By 1920, the world's "below-five child mortality rate" reflected a moderate reduction to 32.1%. But the most impressive declines have occurred in recent decades: by 1970, the death rate had been reduced to 14.49% and in 2015, it reached a historical low of 4.5%. These declines can be observed in many otherwise quite diverse countries. To cite a striking example: South Korea had an estimated mortality rate of 53.2% in 1908, but by 2015, it had declined to a mere 0.3%, a rate below the unimpressive US rate of 0.7% (UNICEF, 2017).

Young children's chances for survival are negatively influenced by parental poverty both within and across countries. Within countries, children born to poor parents tend to be at greater risk than those born to economically better-off parents. Across countries, in some well-to-do societies such as South Korea and Sweden, fewer than 1 out of 300 children die before their fifth birthday. In contrast, the death rates for very poor African countries such as Chad (13.85%) or Nigeria (11.21%) remain unacceptably high even though they have declined quite substantially during the past three decades. The example of a relatively poor country such as India demonstrates that the spread of modern medicine, improved services in the health sector, better-educated citizens such as mothers, and improved sanitary conditions can lead to dramatic results: in 1900, 53.65% or more than half of India's children died before reaching their fifth birthday; by the year 2000, this percentage had declined to 9%, and in 2015, it matched the global rate of 4.5%.

4.2.3 Total Fertility Rates Are Decreasing in Most Countries

Demographers such as Ron Lesthaeghe (2011) have established considerable evidence for the so-called second demographic transition. It traces the shift from prevailing high birth and death rates in preindustrial societies to much lower birth and death rates in industrial and postindustrial societies. Preindustrial societies representing a variety of subsistence economies frequently had TFRs of about five to seven children in the past, but due to their very high death rates, their overall populations tended to increase only slowly or sometimes not at all. This held true, for instance, for Tibetan nomads and for traditional Maya villagers prior to the 1950s.

As modern health practices began to expand in societies such as Indonesia and India in the context of higher per capita incomes, increased literacy rates,

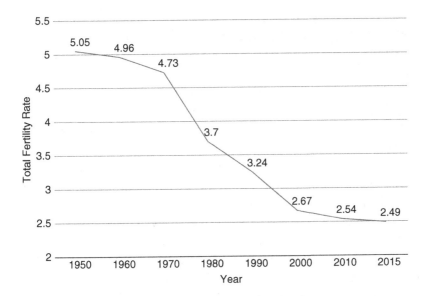

Figure 4.3 Global decline in total fertility rate (TFR), 1950–2015
Sources: Adapted from: Max Roser & Esteban Ortiz-Ospina, *Our World in Data*: Children per Woman & UN Population Division (2017 Revision). https://ourworldindata.org/fertility-rate

and systematic immunization programs, child mortality rates started to decline sharply. The TFRs also began to decline but initially at a slower rate. It is during such a period of still high TFRs but rapidly sinking child mortality rates that a country's population size tends to increase most rapidly, and this has occurred in recent decades in many parts of Asia and Africa. Finally, with continued economic development, higher income levels, modernization, and increasing school attendance, especially by teenage girls, TFRs decline to much lower levels, as demonstrated in all of the world's digital information societies.

Figure 4.3 depicts the decline in global fertility rates between 1950 and 2015. As can be seen, global TFRs in the 1950s and early 1960s hovered around five children, but by 2015, they had declined to half that rate. Such global rates are composed of more than 200 national TFRs, which in 2017 ranged from Niger's very high rate of 6.49 to the astonishingly low rate of 0.83–1.16 for the city-state of Singapore (Central Intelligence Agency, 2018). Yet Niger is a desperately poor country, whereas Singapore has been widely considered an economic success story with few equals. A similar conclusion is suggested by comparing the twelve national TFRs depicted in Table 4.1: ironically, very poor countries such as Nigeria, which rely to various degrees on subsistence agriculture and some instances of nomadic pastoralism, produce by far the most babies per capita whereas the rich, postindustrial information societies are characterized by very low birth rates. In societies with very high child mortality rates and no social security systems, parents may decide to have additional children because they want to ensure that they do not have to face old age and potential destitution by themselves. In addition and as was demonstrated for the Maya families of Xculoc, many hardworking children of peasant families begin to "earn their keep" sometime in their teenage years, thus motivating parents to have more of them.

Rich countries with low birth rates such as South Korea or Germany provide extensive educational opportunities for women, have healthy children and very low child mortality rates, send their children to school while outlawing child labor, and provide women with access to a variety of contraceptives. In this context, providing primary, secondary, and tertiary education for girls and young women appears to have an especially powerful effect on reducing high birth rates (Roser, 2018b). At the same time, an increasing number of women and men are choosing to marry very late or to remain single altogether (Klinenberg, 2013).

4.2.4 Levels of Literacy and Education Are Rising Rapidly, and Especially So For Girls

Figure 4.4 depicts the global rise of literacy levels between 1800 and 2014 (Roser & Ortiz-Ospina, 2018b). Literacy levels are subject to different definitions, not easy to measure, and must be guesstimated for past times. The United Nations Educational, Scientific and Cultural Organization (UNESCO) Institute for Statistics (2017), for instance, sometimes defines literacy as the ability to both read and write a short, simple statement about one's own life – a kind of minimal definition. Literacy levels may also be deduced from statistical data that countries report about their children's enrollment in educational institutions or from parental reports about their children's school attendance. Actual attendance rates, however, may be lower than rates based on enrollment data, especially in the poor countries. Moreover, many children in a good number of countries are taught in an official language that differs from the language they speak at home. Such a situation can lead to poor learning in schools and increased dropout rates. Historians, in turn, may attempt to assess literacy rates by calculating the percentage of people who were able to sign official documents in the past. Altogether, it seems likely that at least some reported literacy rates are overly optimistic and perhaps inflated by a country's desire to "look good." In addition, literacy rates are difficult to compare when different definitions and methodologies are employed to assess them.

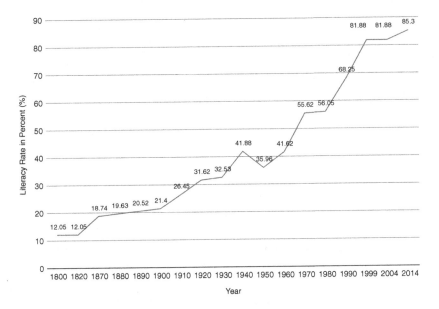

Figure 4.4 Global literacy rates, 1800–2014

Based on: Max Roser & Esteban Ortiz-Ospina (2018b), *Our World in Data*: Literate and Illiterate World Population. https://ourworldindata.org/literacy

In spite of these skeptical remarks, the historical progress revealed in Figure 4.4 is impressive and, at least in its general outlines, real. As late as 1820, only one in eight or nine persons could read and write at least to some degree. Quite a few of these persons lived in Protestant countries, although various Confucian countries such as China and South Korea could boast of important literary traditions, especially for the elite. However, by 1960, the global proportion of literate persons had increased to about four in ten persons, and by 2014, it had again more than doubled to eight and a half in ten persons.

In 2016, 102 million of the world's 750 million illiterate persons aged fifteen years and older were between fifteen and twenty-four years old (UNESCO Institute for Statistics, 2017, table 2.1). That year the literacy rate for male youth (fifteen to twenty-four years) reached 93% and for female youth 90%, and these rates easily surpassed the rates for older persons. Both general literacy rates and rates for youth remain considerably lower in sub-Saharan Africa (e.g., 79% for male youth and 72% for female youth) and moderately lower in southern Asia (91% for male youth and 86% for female youth), when compared to the other world regions.

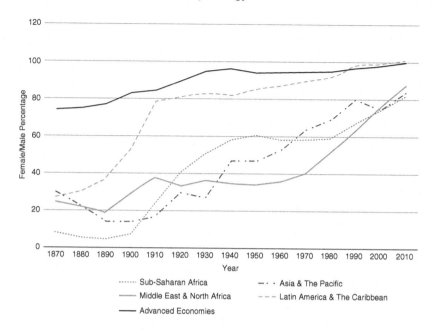

Figure 4.5 Gender ratios for mean years of schooling, 1870–2010
Source: Lee and Lee (2016) & Our WorldInData.org/global-rise-of education
CC BY-SA

In the past few decades, an increasing percentage of school-age children have been attending educational institutions. This progress has been especially striking for girls. Figure 4.5 displays gender ratios for mean years of schooling. A gender ratio of 60%, for instance, indicates that in a given region of the world, the average number of years of schooling for girls is only 60% of the average number of years for male students. The graph shows that in the year 2010, Latin American female students were actually completing a slightly higher number of school years than their male peers whereas no gender difference was reported for European students. In sub-Saharan Africa, Asia and the Pacific, and the Middle East and Africa, we see dramatic improvements over time. Whereas in the late nineteenth century, female students from those regions completed a mere 5% to 25% of the school years of male students, by 2010, this percentage had improved to around 80%. Given that these trends are still continuing, it may be predicted that female and male students will approach global parity around the years 2025–2028. This is good news since women's literacy tends to lead to increased child survival, decreased fertility, better ability to glean important information from the mass media and the Web, better preparation of their children for attending school, improved abilities to deal with bureaucratic health services, and increased awareness of the world outside their families and communities (Gakidu et al., 2010; LeVine et al., 2016). In addition, equal attendance at schools represents a special form of social justice. Nevertheless, in 2016, some 63 million children of school age were still not attending school. Of these, 34 million lived in sub-Saharan Africa and 10 million in South Asia (UNESCO Institute for Statistics, 2018). Many of them came from poor families and were kept out of school because of work responsibilities. In South Asian countries, girls are sometimes taken out of school once they approach puberty because families believe that "something could happen" to them on their way to school, and this would ruin their chances for getting married. Moreover, in some Islamic countries such as Afghanistan and parts of Pakistan, girls may be kept home for religious reasons. This practice tends to reinforce major inequalities between the sexes as well as high fertility rates.

As more and more children attend school, a declining percentage of them are involved in child labor and hazardous work. According to the International Labour Office (2017), in the year 2000, 245.5 million or 16% of the world's children aged five to seventeen years were involved in extensive child labor. By 2016, these numbers had declined to 152 million or 9.6% of the world's children. Even more importantly, whereas in 2000, 11.1% of all children were caught up in hazardous work, this percentage had declined to 4.6% by the year 2016. At the same time keep in mind that it is often difficult to identify abused children, some of whom are subject to commercial sexual exploitation and trafficking in countries such as India (ECPAT, 2018). Others are forced to work in sweatshops, on construction sites, as domestic servants, as child beggars in the streets, or as child soldiers. Thus, some of the reported rates may represent underestimations. Reducing the number of children exposed to such demeaning and hazardous conditions must remain a central goal of international organizations dedicated to improving the welfare of the world's children. Yes, the world has been making progress – and no, we cannot rest on our laurels since so much remains to do.

4.2.5 The Digital Revolution Is Contributing to More Hybrid and Glocal Forms of Identity

The ongoing digital revolution signifies a shift from mechanical and analogue electronic technology to digital electronics and digital record keeping. Emerging in the latter half of the twentieth century, this radical technological change has already had a profound impact on the lives of children and adolescents throughout much of the world. The revolution is both a motor of, and has

Table 4.2 Mobile Phones and Internet Users in 2016

World Regions	Mobile Phones[*]	Internet Users[*]
East Asia and Pacific	109	52
Europe and Central Asia	125	74
• Eastern Europe and Central Asia	129	64
• Western Europe	122	83
Latin America and Caribbean	109	56
Middle East and North Africa	112	48
North America	123	78
South Asia	85	26
Sub-Saharan Africa	75	20
• Eastern and Southern Africa	71	21
• West and Central Africa	80	19
Least Developed Countries	68	16
World	**101**	**46**

[*] Number per 100 population
Source: UNICEF: The State of the World's Children 2017: Children in a Digital World (derived from table 3.3, p. 17)

become a part of, the intensifying process of globalization. That process is driven by international trade, migration, tourism, digitalization that supports the rapid spread of ideas and information, and the ensuing formation of cultures containing a mixture of global, national, and local ingredients. Even though recent political decisions by the US government are putting a damper on the expansion of international trade and migration, the effects of digitalization will continue to be felt among many of the world's teenagers.

Table 4.2 depicts the global use of mobile phones and the Internet in the year 2016. It shows that in many parts of the world, most persons (including many children) are making use of mobile phones in order to keep in steady contact with family members, friends, peers, teachers, and other important persons in their life. Even in the world's poorest and least developed countries, the use of mobile phones has been spreading steadily. In contrast, access to the Internet remains uncommon in such countries. Uneducated rural girls from poor families residing in low-income countries are especially unlikely to go online.

Generally speaking, youth aged fifteen to twenty-four are the most connected group worldwide, with 71% online. Indeed, children and adolescents below the age of eighteen years make up about one-third of all Internet users (UNESCO Institute for Statistics, 2017). Although both parents and the children themselves may worry about the possibility that the latter will be exposed to cyberbullying, unwanted sexual contact, and excessive violence, digital technology enables many of them to gain information about the outside world and expand their horizons. Thus, it provides many opportunities for learning and growing one's network of digitally mediated relationships. This stands in stark contrast to history's preindustrial societies in which many female members in particular would have been poorly informed about the world outside their native village or the village they moved to after their marriage. In contrast, males were traditionally more likely to leave their villages as apprentices, soldiers, monks, merchants, or laborers looking for work elsewhere. Although this gender difference has been declining, it can still be found in some poor communities such as isolated Maya villages.

The forces of globalization have led many of today's children and youth to experience glocalized ways of growing up in which local and global influences become intertwined (Tomlinson, 1999). While their identities remain to various degrees rooted in their existing but expanding social networks and cultures, they are also becoming increasingly aware of their connections to ethnically and culturally diverse national cultures and to the global culture. They may be said to undergo a process of "remote acculturation," i.e., the indirect acquisition of various aspects of faraway cultures in the absence of direct contact with them (Ferguson & Bornstein, 2012). At the same time, local cultures may be both changing and, in part, melting away.

Hybrid experiences and identities occur in many of the world's great cities, where students and adults from quite varied backgrounds intermingle and come under pressure to understand their ethnically and culturally diverse peers and elders, immigrants and minority group members included. At the same time, students residing in such cities are almost always digitally connected. They as well as a growing number of students living in smaller towns are learning to understand computer-generated knowledge, public media, and even some of their computer games within the context of diverse local, national, and global contexts. Since English serves as the dominant language in the world of computers, students in the non-Anglo-Saxon world are frequently encouraged and motivated to acquire English skills and to adopt bicultural frameworks. This helps them to keep up to date and to secure for themselves a better future in an ever more digitalized world. They may watch foreign TV shows, movies, and sports events, interact with immigrant nannies, have dealings with foreign tourists, dress in partly local and partly international ways, desire to work for an international company, hope to become an international soccer star, or participate in church activities guided by missionaries from abroad. Others plan to study abroad when they come of age and are therefore strongly motivated to learn a foreign language and culture from early on. However, many relatively isolated sociocultural "nests" remain, especially for very poor children living in remote rural areas, and such children are in danger of being left behind. A good many of them are unhappily aware of this threat or at least suspect it might exist. Although rural schools in poor nations can be of dubious quality (cf. Lancy, 2015, ch. 9), most of today's children hope to go to school, enjoy the company of their peers, leave behind their parents' world of drudgery, and grow up in a milieu that offers them hope, intellectual challenges, and a better life.

5 Conclusion: Childhoods and Identities in Motion

During recent decades, American and other Western psychologists have conducted many detailed investigations of how children and youth are being raised and coming of age in their own well-to-do societies. In these societies, most children are surrounded by urban environments and live in small families. Whereas full-time labor for young children is illegal, school attendance or homeschooling is mandatory and likely to lead to a protracted period of adolescence. Surrounded by consumerism, a digitalized culture, and same-age friends and peers, their societies' increasingly individualistic ethos encourages adolescents and emerging adults to develop their own visions and dreams for their future. In this context, they typically see arranged marriages as an anachronism, gender roles as subject to major change, and having children as an option competing with other options.

Their perceptions and their lives differ in striking ways from those led by children throughout most of history. Consider, for instance, some essential features of American childhood as it existed around the year 1800 when some 5.3 million persons resided in the United States (Haines, 1994; Hernández, 1994; Mintz, 2006; Wikipedia, 2018b). In those days, about 94% of all white children and their families lived in rural rather than urban areas. At the same time, slavery and relentless toil were the fate of the "Negro" children, who made up roughly a quarter of all children. The average white child had six siblings, although fewer than half of them would reach adulthood – a survival rate not much different from that of India in 1900. From early on the girls helped their mothers to run the family household, took care of younger siblings, fed the chickens, and performed some work in the family garden. Most boys, in turn, were expected to help their fathers in the fields, take care of the family's cattle, and learn how to defend themselves. While many of the predominantly Protestant parents taught their children to read at home, only about a third of them attended school, and that usually only for a few years. Gender roles were often taken for granted and marriages were strongly influenced by economic considerations. In its general outlines, although not in regard to various cultural-religious details, such a childhood hews closer to the childhoods experienced, for instance, by many of Mesoamerica's rural youngsters in the 1950s than to the childhoods experienced by most of today's American high school and college students or those increasingly prevalent in many non-Western countries. Thus, when we study global childhood, we also learn to appreciate some of the shifting ecological, demographic, developmental, and societal underpinnings of American, Western, and world history that otherwise might have remained invisible to our eyes (Stearns, 2017).

In addition, studying long-term trends can help the field of cross-cultural psychology to expand its constricted time horizon so it may grasp more fully the powerful long-term impact of ecological, technological, medical, and demographic forces on human behavior. For instance, cross-cultural psychologists have only rarely studied nomadic pastoralists although theirs has been a basic way of life for thousands of years. In addition, cross-cultural psychology should rely less on data gathered with the help of standardized questionnaires that are, for instance, mostly useless for the study of illiterate nomads, hunters and gatherers, and peasants. Instead, the discipline needs to incorporate interdisciplinary methods, perspectives, and data into its understanding of the human condition and its manifold manifestations across different ways of life.

Because our approach aims to add new ecological, global, and long-term perspectives to the cross-cultural study of children, it diverges from approaches traditionally favored by most psychologists. However, there is no reason why psychologists could not also ask more time-honored questions about the biological, cognitive, emotional, and social development as well as the nature and origins of individual differences among hunter-gatherers, nomadic pastoralists, agriculturalists, and their children. That would require the culture-sensitive adjustment of interview questions, experimental tasks, biological measures, and observational procedures. While this would require considerable ingenuity, time, and effort from researchers, it could also lead to new insights about what is more universal and what is more culture-specific about human development and the various influences shaping it. Moreover, such research would profit from interdisciplinary cooperation together with psychologists' immersion in truly different ways of life. However, academics under pressure to publish articles in high-quality journals may be reluctant to engage in such time-consuming research.

Returning to the children and youth of today's world, it is clear that relentless change is in store for most of them. The change is driven by the forces of technological innovation, international trade, the expansion of multinational corporations, increased migration both within and between societies, international tourism, international education, and the broader currents of globalization. More specifically, for Australia's Aboriginal children, these at times confusing and troubling changes might take the form of education by cultural outsiders, the habitual use of cellphones, exposure to the national and international entertainment culture on TV and the Internet, and perhaps even a future marriage with a white "Aussie bloke." For the increasingly multicultural children of Tibetan nomads, change might consist of solar panels on the top of their tents, becoming aware of a different outside world that is sneaking into their tents as they are watching TV, the negative impact of global warming and overpopulation on the nomadic way of life, and being sent away to an ethnically diverse boarding school located in a town or city. For some of the Maya children of San Pedro, learning English and selling ethnic souvenirs to Western tourists and expatriates might constitute their way of contributing to their families' meager finances while helping to conjure up new visions in their minds. Additional examples include attempting to "make it" for rural teenagers moving to Nigeria's exploding, multiethnic, multireligious, and globally connected city of Lagos; trying to reconcile conflicting interpretations of the Holy Quran with their lives as minority group members in secular and nationalistic France for Arab youngsters from North Africa; and listening to culturally mixed pop music while temporarily trying to forget about endless English lessons and the looming examination hell for South Korean children. At the same time, far fewer of the world's children are dying of traditional childhood diseases, even in the poorer countries, and more girls and boys than ever before are attending school rather than having to engage in demanding and sometimes dangerous child labor from an early age. Thus, global change has led to some very positive consequences for many children, although their lives may also have grown more novel, complex, individualistic (Santos, Varnum, & Grossman, 2017), driven, confusing, and less tied to the soil and the outdoors.

At the same time, the world must confront the powerful implications of the fact that children are multiplying rapidly in the world's poor countries given their sharply declining mortality rates. The projected increase in the world's population for the rest of the twenty-first century could easily lead to very serious consequences in the not-so-distant future since overpopulation is likely to increase the risk for destructive conflicts, both within and between countries. Such conflicts, in turn, frequently result in numerous child deaths and miserable child refugees as may be observed in the present crises in Syria, South Sudan, and Yemen (UNICEF USA, 2018). Moreover, in the coming decades, the ongoing climate crisis is destined to intensify in various destructive ways that even experts cannot fully predict. Overpopulation, increasing global temperatures, disappearing fish and mountains of plastic in the oceans, melting polar ice, shrinking permafrost areas and glaciers in the Tibetan High Plateau, expanding human settlements in the world's forest regions, water shortages in the Middle East and Cape Town, wars and civil wars, and involuntary migrations are liable to feed upon each other in the form of vicious cycles.

On a more positive note and from an action-oriented point of view, the most important long-term plan to improve the global fate of children and adults can be found in the United Nations' seventeen Sustainable Development Goals (SDGs), with Goal #1 quite rightfully being the elimination of extreme poverty everywhere. For children, extreme poverty too often means early death, malnutrition, hunger, exploitative work, no schooling, and premature marriages for girls (Ali & Minoui, 2010). Adopted by the United Nations General Assembly in September 2015, the seventeen goals form the backbone of an ambitious yet also very specific agenda for the years 2016–2030 that the world community has agreed upon. It is aimed at targets such as reducing poverty, hunger, and gender inequality while at the same time improving health, education, and justice. These goals have numerous implications for global child welfare as summarized in the United Nations Children's Fund (UNICEF), 2018. The UN agenda seeks to ensure that every child survives and thrives, goes to school and participates in organized learning, is protected from violence, exploitation, and harmful practices, lives in a safe and clean environment, and has a fair chance in life. In this context, UNICEF has established forty-four child-related indicators that can be used to track the world's progress in improving children's lives. To confront this task is especially important but also quite difficult for the world's poorest and sometimes politically unstable nations, especially in sub-Saharan Africa. We can only hope that the world's richer countries and individuals will demonstrate the will and find the means to support these nations in effective ways because it is there that we can find some of the world's most exploited and miserable children. They deserve our inspired support rather than our disregard for humanitarian values and global human welfare in the service of short-sighted nationalistic and economic goals.

References

Ahmed, R. A., & Gielen, U. P. (2017). Women in Egypt. In C. Brown, U. P. Gielen, J. L. Gibbons, & J. Kuriansky, eds., *Women's Evolving Lives: Global and Psychosocial Perspectives*. New York, NY: Springer, pp. 91–116.

Ali, N., & Minoui, D. (2010). *I Am Nujood, Age 10 and Divorced*. New York, NY: Three Rivers Press.

Arnett, J. J. (1999). Adolescent storm and stress reconsidered. *American Psychologist*, **54**, 317–326.

Atkinson, C. (2009). *The Violence Continuum: Australian Aboriginal Male Violence and Generational Post-Traumatic Stress*. Saarbrücken, Germany: LAP Lambert Academic Publishing.

Australian Institute of Family Studies (2017). *Child Protection and Aboriginal and Torres Strait Islander Children* (CFCA Resource Sheet, August 2017).

Bangsbo, E. (2008). Schooling for knowledge and cultural survival: Tibetan community schools in nomadic herding areas. *Educational Review*, **69**, 69–84.

Bank of Korea. (2018). *Economic Statistics System: 100 Korean STAT – GNI per Capita*. Retrieved on June 25, 2018, from https://ecos.bok.or.kr/EIndex_en.jsp.

Baring, M. (2018). Mongolian herders leave nomadic lifestyle for the city. *Christian Science Monitor*. Retrieved on June 12, 2018, from www .csmonitor.com/Environment/2018/0503/Mongolian-herders-leave-nomadic-lifestyle-for-the-city.

Barry, H., III, Child, I. L., & Bacon, M. K. (1959). Relation of child training to subsistence economy. *American Anthropologist*, **61**(1), 51–63.

Beckwith, C., & Fisher, A. (1999). *African Ceremonies*, 2 vols. New York, NY: Abrams.

Broome, R. (2010). *Aboriginal Australians: A History since 1788*, 4th edn. Crows Nest, Australia: Allen & Unwin.

Buti, T. (2002). The removal of Aboriginal children: Canada and Australia compared. *University of Western Sydney Law Review*, **6**, 25–37.

Byun, T. S. (2014, December 8). 76% of respondents said, "Educational attainments determine one's life": Academic success is still too important. *Hankook Ilbo*. Retrieved on June 24, 2018, from www.hankookilbo .com/v/7bed26d7e0cf4e3aa8be46c01ba7ca66.

Cain, M. T. (1980). The economic activities in Bangladesh. In R. E. Evenson, C. A. Florencio, & F. B. N. White, eds., *Rural Household*

Studies in Asia. Kent Ridge, Singapore: Singapore University Press, pp. 188–217.

Caldwell, B. K., & Caldwell, J. C. (2005). Family size control by infanticide in the great agrarian societies of Asia. *Journal of Comparative Family Studies*, **36**(2), 205–226.

Cameron, N., & Bogin, B. (eds.). (2012). *Human Growth and Development*, 2nd edn. San Diego, CA: Academic Press.

Central Intelligence Agency (CIA). (2018). *The World Factbook*. Available at: www.cia.gov/library/publications/the-world-factbook/.

Chun, J. (2004). Daily schedule for 12th graders: Lifestyles of 12th graders in South Korea. *OhmyNews*. Retrieved on June 24, 2018, from www.ohmynews .com/NWS_Web/Articleview/article_print.aspx?cntn_cd=A0000207861.

Codding, B. F. (2016). *Why Forage? Hunters and Gatherers in the Twenty-First Century*. Albuquerque, NM: University of New Mexico Press.

Correa-Chávez, M., & Rogoff, B. (2009). Children's attention to interactions directed to others: Guatemalan and European American patterns. *Developmental Psychology*, **45**, 630–641.

Cosminsky, S. (2016). *Midwives and Mothers: The Medicalization of Childbirth on a Guatemalan Plantation*. Austin, TX: University of Texas Press.

Dollfus, P. (2013). Transformation processes in nomadic pastoralism in Ladakh. *Himalaya, the Journal of the Association for Nepal and Himalayan Studies*, **32**(1–2), 61–72.

Eickelkamp, U. (2011a). Changing selves in remote Australia? Observations on Aboriginal family life, childhood and "modernization." *Anthropological Forum*, **21**(2), 131–151.

Eickelkamp, U. (ed.). (2011b). *Growing Up in Central Australia: New Anthropological Studies of Aboriginal Childhood and Adolescence*. New York, NY: Berghahn Books.

Ekvall, R. B. (1961). The nomadic patterns of living among the Tibetans as preparation for war. *American Anthropologist*, **63**(6), 1250–1263.

Ekvall, R. B. (1968). *Fields on the Hoof: Nexus of Tibetan Nomadic Pastoralism*. New York, NY: Holt, Rinehart and Winston.

Ember, C. R., & Ringen, E. J. (2017). Childhood. *Human Relations Area Files*. Retrieved on November 19, 2018, from http://hraf.yale.edu/ehc/summaries/ childhood.

End Child Prostitution and Trafficking (ECPAT). (2018). Regional overview: Sexual exploitation of children in Southeast Asia. Retrieved June 18, 2018, from www.ecpat.org/wp-content/uploads/2018/02/ Regional-Overview_Southeast-Asia.pdf.

Ferguson, G. M., & Bornstein, M. H. (2012). Remote acculturation: The "Americanization" of Jamaican islanders. *Child Development*, **83**(5), 1486–1493.

Gakidu, E., Crowling, K., Lozano, R., & Murray, C. J. L. (2010). Increased educational attainment and its effect on child mortality in 175 countries between 1970 and 2009: A systematic analysis. *Lancet*, **376**, 959–974.

Gaskins, S. (2000). Children's daily activities in a Mayan village: A culturally grounded description. *Cross-Cultural Research*, **34**, 375–389.

Gaskins, S. (2003). From corn to cash: Change and continuity within Mayan families. *Ethos*, **31**(2), 248–273.

Gaskins, S. (2006). The cultural organization of Yucatec Mayan children's social interactions. In X. Chen, D. C. French, & B. H. Schneider, eds., *Peer Relationships in Cultural Context*. Cambridge, UK: Cambridge University Press, pp. 283–309.

Gibbons, J. L. (2000). Personal and social development of adolescents: Integrating findings from preindustrial and modern industrialized societies. In A. L. Comunian & U. P. Gielen, eds., *International Perspectives on Human Development*. Lengerich, Germany: Pabst Science Publishers, pp. 403–429.

Gielen, U. P. (1993). Gender roles in traditional Tibetan cultures. In L. L. Adler, ed., *International Handbook on Gender Roles*. Westport, CT: Greenwood, pp. 413–437.

Gielen, U. P. (2016). The changing lives of 2.2 billion children: Global demographics trends and economic disparities. In U. P. Gielen & J. L. Roopnarine, eds., *Childhood and Adolescence: Cross-Cultural Perspectives and Applications*, 2nd edn. Santa Barbara, CA: Praeger, pp. 63–95.

Gielen, U. P., & Roopnarine, J. L. (eds.). (2016). *Childhood and Adolescence: Cross-Cultural Perspectives and Applications*, 2nd edn. Santa Barbara, CA: Praeger.

Goldin, L. R. (2011). *Global Work and Ideology in Rural Guatemala*, 2nd edn. Tucson, AZ: University of Arizona Press.

Greenfield, P. M., Keller, H., Fuligni, A., & Maynard. A. (2003). Cultural pathways through universal development. *Annual Review of Psychology*, **54**, 461–490.

Gurven, M., & Kaplan, H. (2007). Longevity among hunter-gatherers: A cross-cultural examination. *Population and Development Review*, **33**(2), 321–365.

Haines, M. R. (1994). NBR working paper series, *The Population of the United States, 1790–1920*.

Hamilton, A. (1980). Dual social systems: Technology, labour and women's secret rites in the Eastern Western Desert of Australia. *Oceania*, **51**, 4–19. doi:10.1002/j.1834-4461.1980.tb01416.x

Hamilton, A. (1981). *Nature and Nurture: Aboriginal Child-Rearing in North Central Arnhem Land*. Canberra, Australia: Australian Institute of Aboriginal Studies.

Hermanns, M. (1959). *Die Familie der A mdo-Tibeter* [*The Family of the A mdo-Tibetans*]. Freiburg/B., Germany: Verlag Karl Alber.

Hernández, D. J. (1994). Children's changing access to resources: A historical perspective. *Society for Research in Child Development Social Policy Report*, **8**, 1–23.

Hernández, T. (1941). Children among the Drysdale River tribes. *Oceania*, **12**(3), 122–133.

Hewlett, B. S. (ed.). (2014). *Hunter-Gatherers of the Congo Basin: Culture, History and Biology of African Pygmies*. New Brunswick, NJ: Transaction.

Hewlett, B. S., & Lamb, M. E. (eds.). (2005). *Hunter-Gatherer Childhoods: Evolutionary, Developmental and Cultural Perspectives*. New Brunswick, NJ: Transaction.

Institute for Economics and Peace (2016). *Australian Youth Development Index: A Jurisdictional Overview of Youth Development*. Melbourne, Australia: Victoria University. Retrieved on June 5, 2018, from www.documentcloud.org/documents/3010514-Australian-Youth-Development-Index-report.html#document/p2.

International Labour Office. (2017). *Global Estimates of Child Labour: Results and Trends, 2012–2016*. Geneva, Switzerland. Retrieved on May 18, 2018, from www.ilo.org/wcmsp5/groups/public/@dgreports/@dcomm/documents/publication/wcms_575499.pdf.

Isom, J. (2009). Tibet's nomadic pastoralists: Tradition, transformation and prospects. *Indigenous Affairs*, **3–4**, 6–13.

Jarrett, S. (2013). *Liberating Aboriginal People from Violence*. Ballan, Australia: Connor Court Publishing.

Kağitçibaşi, Ç., & Ataca, B. (2005). Value of children and family change: A three-decade portrait from Turkey. *Applied Psychology: An International Review*, **54**(3), 317–337. doi:10.1111/j.1464-0597.2005.00213.x

Kelly, R. L. (2013). *The Lifeways of Hunter-Gatherers: The Foraging Spectrum*. Cambridge, UK: Cambridge University Press.

Kim, E. S. (2018). [Why] "Spring is crazy season" for 8th graders in Daechi-dong. *Chosun Ilbo*. Retrieved on June 23, 2018, from http://news.chosun.com/site/data/html_dir/2018/03/16/2018031601528.html.

Kim, H. (2018). Sixty 4-year colleges may have no freshmen students in 2020: The root of education is being shaken. *MK News*. Retrieved on June 23, 2018, from http://news.mk.co.kr/v7/newsPrint.php?year=2018&no=384292.

Kim, S. W. (2017). President Moon decided the postponement of the national college entrance exam. *Yonhap News*. Retrieved on June 23, 2018, from www.yonhapnews.co.kr/bulletin/2017/11/17/0200000000AKR20171117 051100001.HTML.

Klinenberg, E. (2013). *Going Solo: The Extraordinary Rise and Surprising Appeal of Living Alone*. New York, NY: Penguin.

Korea Consumer Agency. (2015). Research: Private education for elementary students and their expenses. Retrieved on June 24, 2018, from http://data .noworry.kr/130?category=449237.

Korea Health Promotion Institute. (2014). *Research: Adolescents' Perceptions of Health*. Seoul, ROC: Korea Health Promotion Institute.

Korean Educational Development Institute. (2017). *Statistical Yearbook of Education*. Retrieved on June 23, 3018, from http://std.kedi.re.kr/mobile/publ/ publFile?survSeq=2017&menuSeq=3894&publSeq=2&menuCd=70123&me nuId=1_7_7&itemCode=02.

Kramer, K. L. (2005). *Maya Children: Helpers at the Farm*. Cambridge, MA: Harvard University Press.

Lancy, D. F. (2015). *The Anthropology of Childhood: Cherubs, Chattel, Changelings*, 2nd edn. Cambridge, UK: Cambridge University Press.

Larson, R. W., & Verma, S. (1999). How children and adolescents spend time across the world: Work, play, and developmental opportunities. *Psychological Bulletin*, **125**(6), 701–736.

Lee, D. H. (2012). English kindergarten: Children's hell created by parents' greed. *Pressian*. Retrieved on June 22, 2018, from http://m.pressian.com /news/article_print.html?no=40070.

Lee, J.-W., & Lee, H. (2016). Human capital in the long run. *Journal of Development Economics, 122*, 147–169.

Lee, J. Y. (2018). There are 160 English kindergartens in Seoul: Monthly tuition can be up to 1,760,000 KRW (1,760 USD). *Yonhap News*. Retrieved on June 22, 2018, from www.yonhapnews.co.kr/dev/9601000000.html

Lee, R. B. (2012). *The Dobe Ju/'Hoansi*, 4th edn. Belmont, CA: Wadsworth.

Lehmann, P. H., & Ullal, J. (1981). *Tibet: Das stille Drama auf dem Dach der Welt [Tibet: The Quiet Drama on the Roof of the World]*. Hamburg, Germany: Geo.

Lenski, G. (2005). *Ecological-Evolutionary Theory: Principles and Applications*. Boulder, CO: Paradigm Publishers.

Lesthaeghe, R. J. (2011). The "Second Demographic Transition": A conceptual map for the understanding of late modern demographic developments in fertility and family formation. *Historical Social Research*, **36**(2), 179–218.

LeVine, R. A. (1988). Human parental care. *New Directions for Child Development*, **40**, 3–12.

LeVine, R. A., LeVine, S. E., Schnell-Anzola, B., Rowe, M. L., & Dexter, E. (2016). *Literacy and Mothering: How Women's Schooling Changes the Lives of the World's Children*, reprint edn. New York, NY: Oxford University Press.

Lew-Levy, S., Lavi, N., Reckin, R., Cristóbal-Azkarate, J., & Ellis-Davies, K. (2018). How do hunter-gatherer children learn social and gender norms? *Cross-Cultural Research*, **52**(2), 213–255.

Malin, M., Campbell, K., & Agius, L. (1996). *Raising Children in the Nunga Aboriginal Way*. Australian Institute of Family Studies: Family Matters No.43. Retrieved on June 17, 2018, from http://citeseerx.ist.psu.edu/view doc/download?doi=10.1.1.603.791&rep=rep1&type=pdf.

Martinéz-Pérez, M. (2015). Adults' orientation of children – and children's initiative to pitch in – to everyday adult activities in a Tsotsil Maya community. *Advances in Child Development and Behavior*, **49**, 113–135.

Mawhinney, S. E. (2015). Coming of Age: Youth in England, c. 1400–1600. PhD Dissertation, History, University of York, UK.

Maynard, A. E. (2002). Cultural teaching: The development of teaching skills in Maya sibling interactions. *Child Development*, **73**(3), 969–982.

McGlade, H. (2012). *Our Greatest Challenge: Aboriginal Children and Human Rights*. Canberra, Australia: Aboriginal Studies Press.

Miller, D. J. (2007). The world of Tibetan nomads. Retrieved on April 18, 2018, from https://case.edu/affil/tibet/documents/TheWorldofTibetanNomadsSept14.pdf.

Mintz, S. (2006). *Huck's Raft: A History of American Childhood*. Cambridge, MA: Belknap Press.

Nam, J. (2017). Young people think of test scores as the fairest. *Kyunghyang Shinmun*. Retrieved on June 22, 2018, from http://news.khan.co.kr/kh_news/khan_art_view.html?artid=201712182154005.

National Youth Commission. (2005). *Report: Elementary, Middle, and High School Students' Lifestyles for Holidays and after School Hours*. Seoul, ROC: National Youth Commission.

National Youth Policy Institute. (2014). *Statistics for South Korean Children's and Adolescents' Human Rights Situations*. Seoul, ROC: National Youth Policy Institute.

Newton, B. J. (2017). An Aboriginal community's perceptions and experiences of child neglect in a rural town. *Australian Journal of Social Issues*, **52**(3), 62–77.

No Worry. (2014). Research: Private education for mathematics. Retrieved on June 22, 2018, from http://data.noworry.kr/33.

Nolan, P., & Lenski, G. (2014). *Human Societies: An Introduction to Macrosociology*. New York, NY: Oxford University Press.

Nulo, N. (2014). *My Tibetan Childhood: When Ice Shattered Stone*. Durham, NC: Duke University Press.

Oh, K. (2018). Worst study plan mentioned by "Master of Study" Kang S. *SBS News*. Retrieved on June 22, 2018, from https://news.sbs.co.kr/news/endPage.do?news_id=N1004678640.

O'Loughlin, T. (2009). Mixed marriage rates rise in Australia. *The Guardian* (Australia). Retrieved on November 19, 2018, from www.theguardian.com/world/2009/apr/06/aborigines-australia-marriage.

Penman, R. (2006). *The "Growing Up" of Aboriginal and Torres Strait Islander Children: A Literature Review*. Canberra, Australia: Department of Families, Community Services and Indigenous Affairs, Australian Government.

Postiglione, G. A., Jiao, B., & Goldstein, M. C. (2011). Education in the Tibetan Autonomous Region: Policies and practices in rural nomadic communities. In J. Ryan, ed., *Education Reform in China: Changing Concepts, Contexts and Practices*. London, UK: Routledge, pp. 92–109.

Reich, D. (2018). *Who We Are and How We Got Here: Ancient DNA and the New Science of the Human Past*. New York, NY: Pantheon.

Ripley, A. (2011). South Korea: Kids, stop studying so hard! *TIME*. Retrieved on June 22, 2018, from http://content.time.com/time/magazine/article/0,9171,2094427,00.html.

Rogoff, B. (2011). *Developing Destinies: A Mayan Midwife and Town*. New York, NY: Oxford University Press.

Rogoff, B., Sellers, M. J., Pirrotta, S., Fox, N., & White, S. H. (1975). Age of assignment of roles and responsibilities to children. *Human Development*, **18**, 353–369.

Rohner, R. P. (1975). *They Love Me, They Love Me Not: A Worldwide Study of the Effects of Parental Acceptance and Rejection*. New Haven, CT: HRAF Press.

Roscoe, P. (2006). Fish, game, and the foundations of complexity in forager society: The evidence from New Guinea. *Cross-Cultural Research*, **40**(1), 29–46.

Roser, M. (2017). *Fertility.* Retrieved on November 17, 2017, from https://ourworldindata.org/fertility/.

Roser, M. (2018a). *Our world in data.* Available from https://ourworldindata.org/child-mortality.

Roser, M. (2018b). *Fertility Rate.* Retrieved on May 18, 2018, from https://ourworldindata.org/fertility-rate.

Roser, M. (2018c). *Our world in data.* Available from https://ourworldindata.org/

Roser, M., & Ortiz-Ospina, E. (2018b). *Literacy.* Retrieved on May 18, 2018, from https://ourworldindata.org/literacy.

Roser, M., & Ortiz-Ospina, E. (2018a). *World Population Growth.* Retrieved on May 16, 2018, from https://ourworldindata.org/world-population-growth.

Royal Commission and Board of Inquiry into Protection and Detention Systems of the Northern Territories (November 2017). *Report Vols. 1–4 and Media Release.*

Santos, H. C., Varnum, M. E. W., & Grossmann, I. (2017). Global increases in individualism. *Association for Psychological Science,* **28**(9), 1228–1239. doi: 10.1177/0956797617700622

Schlegel, A., & Barry, H., III. (1991). *Adolescence: An Anthropological Inquiry.* New York, NY: Free Press.

Schlesinger, S. C., Kinzer, S., & Coatsworth, J. H. (2005). *Bitter Fruit,* 2nd edn. Cambridge, MA: Harvard University David Rockefeller Center for Latin American Studies.

Schneider, N. (2016). The monastery in a Tibetan pastoralist context: A case study from Kham Minyag. *Études mongoles et sibériennes, centralasiatiques et tibétaines* (online version), 1–18. Retrieved on September 20, 2018, from http://emscat.revues.org/2798.

Secretariat of National Aboriginal and Torres Strait Islander Child Care (SNAICC). (2011). *Growing Up Our Way: Aboriginal and Torres Strait Islander Child Rearing Practices Matrix.* North Fitzroy, Victoria, Australia. Retrieved on July 20, 2018, from www.health.act.gov.au/sites/default/files/SNAICC%20Growing%20up%20our%20way%20Aboriginal%20and%20Torres%20Strait%20Islander%20Child%20Rearing%20Practicestrix.pdf.

Seth, M. J. (2002). *Education Fever: Society, Politics, and the Pursuit of Schooling in South Korea.* Honolulu, HI: University of Hawaii Press.

Seth, M. J. (2010). *A History of Korea: From Antiquity to the Present.* Lanham, MD: Rowman & Littlefield.

Seymour, S. C. (2010). Environmental change, family adaptations, and child development: Longitudinal research in India. *Journal of Cross-Cultural Psychology*, **41**(4), 578–591.

Statistics Korea. (2012). *2017 Statistics for Adolescents: Press Release*. Seoul, ROC: Statistics Korea & Ministry of Gender Equality and Family.

Stollak, I., Valdez, M., Rivas, K., & Perry, H. (2016). *Casas Maternas* in the rural highlands of Guatemala: A mixed-methods case study of the introduction and utilization of birthing facilities by an Indigenous population. *Global Health: Science and Practice*, **4**(1), 114–131.

Stearns, N. P. (2017). *Childhood in World History*, 3rd edn. New York, NY: Routledge.

Tan, G. G. (2017). *In the Circle of White Stones: Moving through Seasons with Nomads of Eastern Tibet*. Seattle, WA: University of Washington Press.

The Economist. (2015). Education in South Korea: The crème de la cram – Korean kids with pushy parents use crammers to get into crammers. *The Economist*. Retrieved on June 25, 2018, from www.economist.com /asia/2015/09/19/the-creme-de-la-cram.

Tomlinson, J. B. (1999). *Globalization and Culture*. Chicago, IL: University of Chicago Press.

United Nations Children's Fund (UNICEF). (2018). *Progress for Every Child in the SDG Era*. Retrieved on May 12, 2018, from www.data .unicef.org.

United Nations Children's Fund (UNICEF). *The State of the World's Children 2016: A Fair Chance for Every Child*. Retrieved on September 22, 2017, from www.unicef.org/sowc2016/.

United Nations Children's Fund (UNICEF). *The State of the World's Children 2017: Children in a Digital World*. Retrieved on May 18, 2018, from www .unicef.org/publications/files/SOWC_2017_ENG_WEB.pdf.

UNICEF, USA. (2018). *Syrian Crisis*. Retrieved on May 21, 2018, from www .unicefusa.org/mission/emergencies/child-refugees/syria-crisis.

UNICEF Global Databases (data.unicef.org): *Education: Primary Net Attendance Ratio – Percentage*. Retrieved on June 18, 2018, from https:// data.unicef.org/topic/education/primary-education/.

United Nations Educational, Scientific and Cultural Organization (UNESCO) Institute for Statistics (2017). *Fact Sheet No. 45: Literacy Rates Continue to Rise from One Generation to the Next*. Retrieved on June 18, 2018, from http:// uis.unesco.org/sites/default/files/documents/fs45-literacy-rates-continue-rise-generation-to-next-en-2017_0.pdf.

United Nations Educational, Scientific and Cultural Organization (UNESCO) Institute for Statistics (2018). *Fact Sheet No. 48*. Downloaded on June 22, 2018 from http://uis.unesco.org/sites/default/files/documents/fs48-one-five-children-adolescents-youth-out-school-2018-en.pdf

United Nations General Assembly. (1989). *Convention on the Rights of the Child*. Retrieved on November 19, 2018, from www.ohchr.org/EN/ProfessionalInterest/Pages/CRC.aspx.

United Nations Population Division (2017). Marriage Data 2017. Retrieved on June 7, 2018, from www.un.org/en/development/desa/population/theme/marriage-unions/WMD2017.shtml.

Volk, A. A., & Atkinson, J. A. (2013). Infant and child death in the human environment of evolutionary adaptation. *Evolution and Human Behavior*, **34**, 182–192.

Whiting, B. B., & Edwards, C. (1988). *Children of Different Worlds: The Formation of Social Behavior*. Cambridge, MA: Harvard University Press.

Wikipedia. (2018a). Agriculture. Retrieved on May 16, 2018, from https://en.wikipedia.org/wiki/Agriculture.

Wikipedia. (2018b). 1800 United States Census. Retrieved on June 7, 2018, from https://en.wikipedia.org/wiki/1800_United_States_Census.

World Economic Forum & INSEAD. (2016). The Global Information Technology Report 2016: Innovating in the Digital Economy. S. Baller, S. Dutta, & B. Lanvin, eds. Geneva, Switzerland: World Economic Forum & INSEAD. Retrieved on June 25, 2018, from www.weforum.org/gitr.

Yoo, S. (2017). [2018 College Entrance Exam]. The number of test takers reduced by 12,460, while re-takers increased by 2,412. *Study News: Internet Newspaper for College Entrance Exam*. Retrieved on June 25, 2018, from www.studynews.net/2017/09/13/.

Yu, S. (2017). One out of ten 4~6th graders are addicted to smartphones, female students more. *Joongang Ilbo*. Retrieved on June 25, 2018, from news.joins.com/article/print/21976298.

Zeller, A. C. (1987). A role for women in hominid evolution. *Man*, **22**(3), 528–557.

Acknowledgments

We would like to express our gratitude to Kenneth Keith, Michele Hirsch, Tahereh Ziaian, and an anonymous reviewer for their perceptive comments. Special thanks are also due to Carmelinda Coppola and Kunjal Darji, assistants at the Institute for International and Cross-Cultural Psychology, for their careful work.

Cambridge Elements ≡

Psychology and Culture

Kenneth D. Keith

University of San Diego

Kenneth D. Keith is author or editor of more than 160 publications on cross-cultural psychology, quality of life, intellectual disability, and the teaching of psychology. He was the 2017 president of the Society for the Teaching of Psychology.

About the Series

Elements in Psychology and Culture features authoritative surveys and updates on key topics in cultural, cross-cultural, and indigenous psychology. Authors are internationally recognized scholars whose work is at the forefront of their subdisciplines within the realm of psychology and culture.

Cambridge Elements ≡

Psychology and Culture

Printed in the United States
By Bookmasters